The Three Distinct Knocks
along with
Jachin and Boaz

by Samuel Pritchard

Foreword by
Michael R. Poll

A Cornerstone Book

The Three Distinct Knocks
along with
Jachin and Boaz
by Samuel Pritchard
Foreword by
Michael R. Poll

A Cornerstone Book
Published by Cornerstone Book Publishers
Copyright © 2020 by Michael R. Poll

Cornerstone Book Publishers
New Orleans, LA
www.cornerstonepublishers.com
1cornerstonebooks@gmail.com

First Cornerstone Edition – 2020

Foreword

Speculative Freemasonry was born out of the desire to preserve the philosophical and moral teachings of the old Operative Freemasons. The old "workers in stone" were not only builders of cathedrals, but also builders of humanity. They took good, decent candidates and with the education necessary to give them the skills of Master Builders, they also provided them with the path to becoming better human beings. It was this additional training that was felt to be of such great value to the whole of humanity when the building trades began to decline and the lodges of Operatives began to fade away. The loss of this philosophical education was felt to be unacceptable.

The Renaissance led into the Age of Enlightenment. It was times of great change and self-discovery. Men with no desire at all to enter the building trade, found great value in the moral lessons of the old Operatives. Slowly, these non-Operatives began to find their way into the lodges which once only admitted actual builders or builders in training. While these new members possessed no interest in learning building, they found great wisdom in the lessons of life. They were also intrigued by the ritualistic way these lessons were delivered. With the flavor of alchemy and every science known to man, these ethical plays were provided in a manner to offer the members a chance at spiritual and moral growth. This amazing approach to imparting enlightenment could not be allowed to die along with the building guilds. *Speculative Freemasons* began to save the heart and metaphysical soul of the old Operatives.

Because of the true hunger society possessed for inner growth, the Masonic manner of teaching struck a chord within all who became aware of Speculative Freemasonry's existence. Lodges of Speculative Freemasons soon popped up all over

Europe and then all over the world. The ritual used to deliver the lessons soon evolved to reflect the nature of the societies using the rituals.

In 1723, a London newspaper published what would seem to be the very first Masonic exposure. In 1760, Samuel Pritchard expanded the untitled work to include the opening and closing of the lodge and released the exposure as *The Three Distinct Knocks*. Offered in this book is a digitally enhanced photographic reproduction of the 1760 edition of Pritchard's work. This is a significant work for all Masons, as it provides us with a clear look at the early roots of our Masonic ritual. Along with this publication, is Pritchard's 1797 companion piece, *Jachin and Boaz*.

Masonic ritual is the vehicle used by Freemasonry to deliver the symbolic lessons presented to the candidates. Over time, these rituals, or lessons, are changed, tweaked, modified and molded to match the times and societies where they are used. While the core of the lessons remain the same, the packaging is often varied. Cornerstone is proud to present this important work for your examination and study.

Michael R. Poll
Cornerstone Book Publishers

The Three Distinct Knocks

THE

Three diſtinct Knocks,

Or the Door of the moſt

ANTIENT FREE-MASONRY,

Opening to all Men,

Neither Naked nor Cloath'd,

Bare-foot nor ſhod, &c.

Being an Univerſal Deſcription of all its Branches,

FROM

Its firſt Riſe to this preſent Time,

As it is deliver'd in all Lodges :

CONTAINING,

I. The Author's Reaſons for opening the Door of Maſonry to all the World.

II. How to open a Lodge and ſet the Men to Work.

III. Giving an exact Account of all their Proceedings in the making a Brother, with the Three Obligations or Oaths belonging to the Firſt, Second, and Third Degrees of Maſonry, viz. The Enter'd Apprentice, and Fellow-Craft, and Maſter-Maſon ; with the Obligation belonging to the Chair, and the Gripe and Word.

IV. The Form of a Lodge ; with a full Deſcription of the drawing upon the Floor of a Lodge, with the Three Steps, and a Prayer uſed at the making of a Brother; with Songs to be ſung after grave Buſineſs is done.

V. The Examination of a Brother, whereby he may get Admittance into a Lodge, without going through the Obligations : With all the Words explained that belongs to the Gripe.

VI. A new and accurate Liſt of all the ENGLISH regular Lodges in the World, according to their Seniority, with the Dates of each Conſtitution and Days of Meeting.

By *W—— O—— V—— n :*

Member of a Lodge in *England* at this Time.

The SEVENTH EDITION.

LONDON:

Printed for H. SERJEANT, without *Temple-Bar.*

✹✹✹✹✹✹✹✹✹✹✹✹ ✹✹✹✹✹✹✹✹✹

THE

EXPLANATION

OF THE

FOLLOWING FIGURE,

which is all the

Drawing that is ufed in this Sort of Mafonry,

C A L L E D,

The Most ANTIENT by the *Irifhmen*.

I T is generally done with Chalk, or Charcoal, on the Floor ; that is the Reafon that they want a Mop and Pail fo often
as they do : before when a Man has been made
a Mafon, they wafh it out : but People have
taken Notice, and made Game of them about
the Mop and Pail : So fome Lodges ufe Tape
and little Nails to form the fame Thing, and

a fo

2

ſo keep the World more ignorant of the Matter.

Note. This Plan is drawn on the Floor, Eaſt and Weſt : The Maſter ſtands in the Eaſt, with the Square about his Neck, and the Bible before him, which he takes up and walks forward to the Weſt, near the firſt Step of an oblong Square; where he kneels down, in order to give that ſolemn Obligation to him that has already knelt down, with his Left-knee bare, bent upon the firſt Step; his Right-foot forms a Square, with his naked Right-hand upon the holy Bible, &c.

And ſo to the Second and Third Degree of Maſonry; as is ſhewn upon the Steps.

THE

※※※※※※※※※※※※※※※ ※※※※※※※※※※※

N O T E.

ALL this Figure is wafhed out with a Mop, as aforefaid, as foon as he has received the Obligation.

Then a Table is put in the Place where this Figure was, and they all fit round it; but every Man fitteth in the fame Place as he ftood before the Figure was wafhed out, *viz.* the Mafter in the Eaft, the Senior Warden in the Weft, *&c.*

Every Man has a Glafs fet him, and a large Bowl of Punch, or what they like, is fet in in the Center of the Table; and the Senior Deacon charges (as they call it) in the North and Eaft, and the Junior Deacon in the South and Weft; for it is their Duty fo to do, *i. e.* to fill all the Glaffes.

Then the Mafter takes up his Glafs, and gives a Toaft to the King and the Craft, with Three Times Three in the Prentice's; and

they

they all fay Ditto, and drink all together, minding the Mafter's Motion : They do the fame with the empty Glafs, that he doth ; that is, he draws it a-crofs his Throat Three Times (which is the Penalty of the Obligation of your Throat being cut a-crofs), and then makes Three Offers to put it down : At the Third, they all fet their Glaffes down together, which they call firing : Then they hold the Left-hand Breaft-high, and clap Nine Times with the Right, their Foot going at the fame Time : When this done, they all fit down.

THE

XXXXXXXXXXXXXXXXXXXXXXXXX

THE

Author's REASONS for opening the Door of MASONRY to all the World.

DEDICATED TO

THE RIGHT WORSHIPFUL

COMPANY OF FAITHFUL

IRISH MASTERS

Of Number I,

And the whole FRATERNITY, which it may be of Service to ———

SIRS,

I Am obliged to dedicate my Book to Number I, becaufe they are all Mafters, and in Partnerfhip; befides, they would be angry if I did not give them that Honour; for they that are not Mafters, can't be admitted: But it may be of Service to the younger Brothers, becaufe it will let them into the Tricks that are carried on, which you can't come at under Six or Seven Years, and the Expence of a great many Pounds; but here you may learn it all in a Month, and go and lecture as well as the beft of them. But

B   if

if you belong to any Lodge, you muft give a Shilling every Quarter to Number I, to feaft their d—mn'd Guts, and perhaps your family wanted it at home: But this Family of *Pluto*'s have the impudence of the D—l, to fay if you don't fend a Shilling when they want it, you fhall be excluded all Lodges whatfoever: And thus there goes Four or Five Shillings a Year, you don't know for what; befides other Expences, which is ten times as much. I could give you a Lift of Expences for one Year only would make you ftare; but it does not fignify, for any Man that has been a Mafon Half a Year, and comes to read this Book, will know what I fay to be true, and more fo if he reads it out; for it will let him into things he never thought of, but now he will fee them as plain as pof-fible.

Pray, Brother, what is the matter that Six or Eight or Ten Brethren, that like to learn Mafonry, can't meet at a Brother's Houfe when they pleafe, and fpend their Sixpence with Plea-fure, and depart in Peace, without wrangling and cheating one another; which two often happens of late, by admitting of bad Men, and laying Charges upon them that are not honeft enough to keep one Tittle thereof; which I could fpeak of Two or Three who were made Mafters very lately, and in a Month's Time turned out the moft forfworn Villains in the World.

There-

[3]

Therefore I advife all young Brethren to meet as aforefaid; firft at one Brother's Houfe, and then at another, that is, in the public Way: For what Occafion have you to be confin'd to any particular Lodge, when you may hold a Lodge where you pleafe, and when you pleafe; having either Three, Five, Seven or Eleven, and as many more as you pleafe; and thus you will be of Service to one another, without fending your Money to the grand Number I, as they call it, which they tell you is for Charity; but if it be, I am afraid they make themfelves the Poor: Thus I advife you further, that you have nothing to do with them, for they are Wolves in Sheeps Cloathing.

It was the cuftom among the Primitive Ma-fons, and alfo among the Primitive Chriftians, to vifit one another; for it is faid as Iron fharpens Iron, fo fhall one Man fharpen another.

But methinks I hear fome young Brethren fay, Who fhall inftruct us? I anfwer: Buy this Book, thou wilt have Inftructions enough. But per-haps you will fay, How fhall I know that it is right? Get fome faithful *Irifhman*, for Two or Three Times, and you will foon fee that this Book is right; for they all underftand Mafonry, even the loweft Clafs of them, if they are once made; for then it is the chief of their Bufi-nefs. In the Winter they have a little Money out of

B 2   the

(4)

the Box of Number I, to buy them a few Cloaths, fo you may have one of them any Night, only paying for what he eats and drinks, for they never pay any thing; but if they can lay hold of the Money, they will: So I charge you to take care of that, and you may do well enough with them, paying their Expences of the Night: Or you may have a faithful Inftructor from Number I; the Secretary, or the like, with One or Two with him; but they muft be all free; becaufe they come to inftruct the young Brethren; and fometimes you muft pay a Coach-hire or Waterage, or the like, according to the Situation of the Place.

Therefore it is the beft way not to be troubl'd with them, but as little as you can help; yet I would have you try, and you will find what I fay to be true; for it is by Experience. I could fay ten times more, but I don't care to be too harfh: I only give you Hints, whereby, with a little Experience, you will find it all out; and a great deal more Villainy that is carry'd on, and three Parts of the Free-Mafons know nothing about the Matter.

For they pretended to fo much Holinefs at firft when I came to *England*, I thought they were Gods, but I foon found them D---ls. For at firft I found all their pretended Friendfhip not to be real, becaufe they had fo much of it that made me fick, and I dare fay fome of you, Brethren,

(5)

thren, have been as fick with their pretended Ho-
nefty, as ever I was.

But with all their Wit, they never could find
me out, that I never was made a Mafon, or received any of the following Obligations ; yet I
have been a Member of feveral Lodges, both
Antient and Modern, and Royal Arch ; and have
been Mafter of fome Lodges in *England*. I will
tell you how I came at it without being made ; as
follows.

I am a *German*, born near *Berlin* ; and being
acquainted with an *English* Family, who had a
large Quantity of Books, and being intimate with
their Children, I learnt a little *English*, and took
great delight in reading of *English* Books, which
I could have when I would. About the Year
1740, (I was then upwards of 20 Years old) as I
was looking in my Neighbour's Library, I found
a Pamphlet, called, *Maffonry Diffected*, an *English*
Book ; I read it with great Attention, becaufe I had
heard of Mafonry to be a very bad Thing ; fo I
took great Notice of this Book, and could fay it
all by Heart, or very near, and concluded it was
the whole Thing, but it was not, yet there was
enough to get Admittance into a Lodge. For,

About Two or Three Years after, I went to
Paris ; I had not been there long, before I work'd
with a Man that was a Mafon, and belonged to a
Lodge

(6)

Lodge in *Paris*. We fell in Difcourfe about Mafonry, (I had heard that he he was one before) I afk'd him if he was a Free Mafon; he faid, are you? I faid I am; and he afk'd me where I was made, I faid at *Berlin*. He afk'd me fome Queftions, which I anfwer'd out of the Book, and happen'd to be right; fo he fhook me by the Hand and call'd me Brother, and took me to his Lodge, which I became a Member of, and belong'd to it whilft I ftaid there, which was two or three Years; then my Bufinefs led me to *England*. When I fet out, they gave me a Certificate, and was very forry to part from me, but defir'd me to remember them to all Brothers in *England*, which I did not forget. I went to a Modern Lodge, as the *Irifh* call them, whofe grand Lodge is held at the *Devil* Tavern, but I don't care to mention the Lodge. They never difputed me when I fhew'd them my Certificate, for they were fond of hearing how Mafons proceeded in other Countries, which is juft the fame as it is here, only one Thing in the Mafter's Part, and that I fhall fpeak of in the Mafter's Part. Then I was invited to an *Irifh* Lodge, that call'd themfelves the moft antient Mafons, that holds their Grand Lodge at the *Five Bell* Tavern in the *Strand*, which is the whole Subject of this Book; for which Reafon, their impudent blundering *Irifh* (*T---m T---dman*'s Cart driving) Secretary, have thought fit to ufe fuch Scurrility, to depreciate it in his nonfenfical ftupid performance, called, *A----n R--·n*: But the other I don't meddle

with

(7)

with, becaufe there is a Book already publifhed, call'd *Mafonry Diffected*, which was publifhed in the Year 1700; and I believe was all the Mafonry that was made ufe of of at that Time, but it is not half that is ufed now, tho' it is the nigheft that ever was wrote about the Matter before this.

Although there have been many Books writ about Mafonry, but moft to draw the Reader's Mind from off the aforefaid Book; for I have read them all that have been publifh'd thefe Twenty Years, and I never faw any Mafonry but in the aforefaid Book. There is one publifh'd, called, *A Mafter-Key to Free Mafonry*, but it is not the Thing, tho' it is fomething about the Matter, but fo very little, that it is not worth fpeaking of; there is not one Thing right, only fome of the Words, but not in their proper Places. I wonder that any Man can pretend to write a Book of a Thing that he knows nothing of, but by picking a Bit here there. For no Man is able to fpeak or write this Secret, without he has vifited Lodges fome Years. He fpeaks of Drawing upon the Cieling with a Pencil, that fhews he knew nothing about the Matter, to fill People's Cielings full of Marks and Scratches, which would foon be known to all the World. All Men that ever faw any Thing of Mafonry, knows that their Drawing is upon the Floor, (and that is the Reafon of the Mop and Pail) but any Man that reads my Book with Attention, will find it right, by his own Judgment only;

(8)

only ; for I will affure you there was never fuch an exact Account before publifh'd; which I hope will give entire Satisfaction to all Lovers of Truth; fo I fhall remain,

Your moft obedient

Humble Servant,

W—— O—— V——n.

N. B. *The Stile of the aforefaid and following A-pologies may not be fo fine as it fhould, but I hope the Reader will excufe me, as I am not an* Englifhman ; *but I affure you, my Mean-ing is Truth and Juftice, and I hope will be underftood.*

THE

(9)

THE
Three diſtinct Knocks,

Or the Door of the moſt
ANTIENT FREE-MASONRY,
Opening to all Men, &c.

How to open the Lodge, to ſet the Men to work.

Maſter, to the junior Deacon.

WHAT is the chief care of a Maſon?
Anſwer. To ſee that his Lodge is tyl'd.
Maſ. Pray do your Duty.

N. B. The junior Deacon goes and gives Three
Knocks at the Door; and if there is no-
body nigh, the Tyler without anſwereth
with Three Knocks: The junior Deacon
tells the Maſter, and ſays; Worſhipful,
the Lodge is tyl'd.

C

Maſ.

Maſ. to jun. Dea. The junior Deacon's Place in the Lodge?

Deacon's Anſ. At the Back of the ſenior Warden, or at his Right hand if he permits him.

Maſ. Your Buſineſs?

Deacon's Anſ. To carry Meſſages from the ſenior to the junior Warden, ſo that they may be diſperſed round the Lodge.

Maſ. to the ſen. Dea. The ſenior Deacon's Place in the Lodge?

Sen. Deacon's Anſ. At the Back of the Maſter, or at his Right-hand if he permits him.

Maſ. Your Buſineſs there?

Sen. Deacon's Anſ. To carry Meſſages from the Maſter to the ſenior Warden.

Maſ. The junior Warden's Place in the Lodge?

Deacon's Anſ. In the South.

Maſ. to the jun. Warden. Your Buſineſs there?

Sen. Warden's Anſ. The better to obſerve the Sun, at high Meridian, to call the Men off from Work to Refreſhment, and to ſee that they come on in due Time, that the Maſter may have Pleaſure and Profit thereby.

Maſ. The ſenior Warden's Place in the Lodge?

Jun. Warden's Anſ. In the Weſt.

Maſ. to the ſen. Warden. Your Buſineſs there?

Sen. Warden's Anſ. As the Sun ſets in the Weſt to cloſe the Day, ſo the Senior ſtands in the Weſt to cloſe the Lodge, paying the Hirelings their Wages, and diſmiſſing them from their Labour.

Maſ. The Maſter's Place in the Lodge?

Sen. Warden's Anſ. In the Eaſt.

Maſ. His Buſineſs there?

Sen. Warden's Anſ. As the Sun riſes in the Eaſt

to

(11)

o open the Day, fo the Mafter ftands in the Eaft
o open his Lodge to fet Men to Work.

N. B. Then the Mafter takes off his Hat, which
he always has on but at this Time, and puts
it on again as foon as the Lodge is open
but all the reft keep theirs off, and he de3
clares the Lodge open as follows.

Maf. This Lodge is open, in the Name of God
and holy St. *John,* forbidding all curfing and fwear-
ing, whifpering, and all prophane Difcourfe whatfoever, under no lefs Penalty than what the Majority
fhall think proper; not lefs than One Penny a
Time, nor more than Sixpence.

N. B. Then he gives Three Knocks upon the Table with a wooden Hammer, and puts on
his Hat; then they all fit down, and begin their Lecture, as follows.

The enter'd Aprentice's Lecture.

Maf. BRother, Is there any Thing between you
and I ?

Anf. There is, Wotfhipful.

Maf. What is it Brother ?

Anf. A Secret.

Maf. What is it that Secret, Brother ?

Anf. Mafonry.

Maf. Then I prefume you are a Mafon ?

Anf. I am fo taken and accepted amongft Brothers and Fellows.

Maf. Pray what Manner of Man ought a Mafon Man to be ?

Anf. A Man that is born of a Free Woman.

C 2 *Maf.*

Maf. Where was you firft prepar'd to be made a Mafon ?

Anf. In my Heart.

Maf. Where was you next prepar'd ?

Anf. In a Room adjoining to the Lodge.

Maf. How was you prepar'd Brother ?

Anf. I was neither naked nor cloathed, barefoot nor fhod, depriv'd of all Metal, hoodwink'd with a cable Tow about my Neck, where I was led to the Door of the Lodge in a halting moving Pofture, by the Hand of a Friend, whom I afterwards found to be a Brother.

Maf. How did you know it to be a Door, you being blinded ?

Anf. By finding a Stoppage, and afterwards an Enterance or Admittance.

Maf. How got you Admittance ?

Anf. By three diftinct Knocks.

Maf. What was faid to you within ?

Anf. Who comes there.

Maf. Your Anfwer Brother ?

Anf. One who begs to have and receive Part of the Benefit of this right worfhipful Lodge, dedicated to St. *John,* as many Brothers and Fellows have done before me.

Maf. How do you expect to obtain it ?

Anf. By being free born and well reported.

Maf. What was faid to you then ?

Anf. Enter.

Maf. How did you enter, and upon what ?

Anf. Upon the Point of a Sword or Spear, or fome Warlike Inftrument, prefented to my left naked Breaft.   *Maf.*

(13)

Maſ. What was ſaid to you then ?

Anſ. I was aſk'd if I felt any Thing.

Maſ. What was your Anſwer ?

Anſ. I did, bnt I could ſee nothing.

Maſ. You have told me how you was received, pray who received you ?

Anſ. The Junior Warden.

Maſ. How did he diſpoſe of you ?

Anſ. He deliver'd me to the Maſter, who order'd me to kneel down and receive the Benefit of a Prayer.

Brethren, let Pray.

O Lord God, thou great and univerſal Maſon of the World, and firſt Builder of Man, as it were a Temple ; be with us, O Lord, as thou haſt promiſed, when two or three are gathered together in thy Name, thou wilt be in the midſt of them; be with us, O Lord, and bleſs all our Undertakings, and grant that this our Friend, may become a faithful Brother. Let Grace and Peace be multiplied unto him, through the Knowledge of our Lord Jeſus Chriſt : And grant, O Lord, as he putteth forth his Hand to thy Holy Word, that he may alſo put forth his Hand to ſerve a Brother but not to hurt himſelf or his Family ; that whereby may be given to us great and precious Promiſes, that by this we may be Partakers of thy divine Nature, and having eſcaped the Corruption that is in the World, through Luſt.

O Lord God, add to our Faith Virtue, and to Virtue Knowledge, aud to Knowledge Temperance, and to Temperance Prudence, and to Prudence Patience,

(14)

Patience, and to Patience Godlinefs, and to Godlinefs Brotherly Love, and to Brotherly Love, Charity; and grant, O Lord, that Mafonry may be bleft
throughout the World, and thy Peace be upon us,
O Lord; and grant that we may be all united as
one, through our Lord Jefus Chrift, who liveth and
reigneth for ever and ever. *Amen.*

Maf. After you had received this Prayer, what
was faid to you ?

Anf. I was afk'd who I put my Truft in.

Maf. Your Anfwer Brother ?

Anf. In God.

Maf. What was the next Thing faid to you ?

Anf. I was taken by the Right-hand, and he faid,
rife up and follow your Leader, and fear no Danger.

Maf. After all this how was you difpofed of ?

Anf. I was led Three Times round the Lodge.

Maf. Where did you meet with the firft Oppofition ?

Anf. At the Back of the junior Warden in the
South, where I gave the fame three Knocks as at
the Door.

Maf. What Anfwer did he give you ?

Anf. He faid, who comes there.

Maf. Your Anfwer ?

Anf. The fame as at the Door, one who begs to
have and receive, &c.

Maf. Where did you meet with the fecond Oppofition ?

Anf. At the Back of the Senior Warden in
the Weft, where I made the fame Repetition as
at

(15)

at the Door. He faid, who comes here? One who begs to have and receive, &c.

Maf. Where did you meet with the third Oppofition?

Anf. At the Back of the Mafter in the Eaft, where I made the Repetition as before.

Maf. What did the Mafter do with you?

Anf. He order'd me back to the Senior Warden in the Weft, to receive Inftrnctions.

Maf. What was the Inftructions he gave you?

Anf. He taught me to take one Step upon the firft Step of a right Angle oblong Square, with my left Knee bare bent, my Body upright, my right Foot forming a Square, my naked Right-hand upon the Holy Bible, with the Square and Compafs thereon, my Left-hand fupporting the fame; where I took that folemn Obligation or Oath of a Mafon.

Maf. Brother, Can you repeat that Obligation?

Anf. I will do my Endeavour, with your Affiftance, Worfhipful.

Maf. Stand up and begin.

Anf.   I. W------ V-------,

Of my own free Will and Accord, on in the Prefence of Almighty God, and this right worfhipful Lodge, dedicated to St. *John*, do hereby and hereon moft folemnly and fincerely fwear, that I will always hail, conceal, and never will reveal any of the fecret Myfteries of Free Mafonry, that fhall be deliver'd to me now, or any Time hereafter, except it be to a true and lawful Brother, or in a juft and lawful Lodge of Brothers and Fellows, him or them whom

(16)

whom I fhall find to be fuch, after juft Trial and due Examination.

I furthermore do fwear, that I will not write it, print it, cut it, paint it or ftint it, mark it, ftain it, or engrave it, or caufe fo be done, upon any Thing moveable or immoveable, under the Canopy of Heaven, whereby it may become legible or intellegible, or the leaft Appearance of the Character of a Letter, whereby the fecret Art may be unlawfully obtain'd. All this I fwear, with a ftrong and fteady Refolution to perform the fame, without any Hefitation, mental Refervation, or Self-evafion of Mind in me whatfoever, under no lefs Penalty than to have my Throat cut acrofs, my Tongue torn out by the Root, and that to be buried in the Sands of the Sea, at Low-Water Mark, a Cable's Length from the Shore, where the Tide ebbs and flows twice in Twenty-four Hours ; fo help me God, and keep me ftedfaft, in this my enter'd Apprentices Obligation.

[*He kiffes the Book.*]

Funde merum Genio.

N. B. After this Obligation they drink a Toaft to the Heart that conceals, and to the Tongue that never reveals.

The Mafte; in the Chair gives it, and they all fay Ditto, and they draw the Glaffes acrofs their Throats as aforefaid.

Maf. Now Brother, after you received this Obligation, what was the firft that was faid to you ?

Anf.

(17)

Anf. I was afk'd what I moft defir'd ?

Maf. What was your Anfwer ?

Anf. To be brought to Light.

Maf. Who brought you to Light ?

Anf. The Mafter and the reft of the Brethren.

Maf. When you was thus brought to Light, what were the firft Things you faw ?

Anf. Bible, Square and Compafs.

Maf. What was it they told you they fignified ?

Anf. Three great Lights in Mafonry ?

Maf. Explain them, Brother.

Anf. The Bible, to rule and govern our Faith ; the Square, to Square our Actions ; the Compaffes is to keep us within Bounds with all Men, particularly with a Brother.

Maf. What were the next Things that were fhewn to you ?

Anf. Three Candles, which I was told were Three Leffer Lights in Mafonry.

Maf. What do they reprefent ?

Anf. The Sun, Moon, and Mafter-Mafon.

Maf. Why fo, Brother ?

Anf. There is the Sun to rule the Day, the Moon to rule the Night, and the Mafter-Mafon's Lodge, or at leaft ought fo to do.

Maf. What was then done to you ?

Anf. The Mafter took me by the Right-hand, and gave me the Gripe and Word of

D   an

(18)

an enter'd Apprentice, and said, Rife up Brother BOAZ.

N. B. Sometimes they shew you the Sign before this Gripe and Word is given, which is BOAZ : It is the enter'd Apprentice's Word, and the Gripe thereto belonging is to pinch with your Right-thumb Nail, upon the firft Joint of your Brother's Right-hand.

Maf. Have you got this Gripe and Word, Brother ?

Anf. I have, Worfhipful

Maf. Give it to your next Brother.

N. B. Then he takes his next Brother by the Right-hand, and gives him the Gripe and Word, as before defcribed : he tells the Mafter, that is right.

According to the following Proof.

The 1ft. Brother gives him the Gripe.
The 2d. Brother fays, What's this ?
1ft. *Bro.* The Gripe of an enter'd Apprentice,
2d. *Bro.* Has it got a Name ?
1ft. *Bro.* It has.
2d. *Bro.* Will you give it me ?
1ft. *Bro.* I'll letter it with you, or halve it.
2d. *Bro.* I'll halve it with you.
1ft. *Bro.* Begin.
2d. *Bro.* No, you begin firft.
1ft. *Bro.* BO-
2d. *Bro.* A Z :
1ft. *Bro.* B O A Z.
2d. *Bro.* It is right, worfhipful Mafter.

Maf.

23

(19)

Maſ. What was the next Thing that was ſhewn to you ?

Anſ. The due Guard, or Sign, of an enter'd Apprentice.

N. B. The due Guard or Sign, as they call it, is by drawing your Right-hand a-croſs your Throat edgeways, which is to put you in mind of the Penalty of your Obligation ; that you would ſooner have your Throat cut a-croſs, than diſcover the Secrets of Maſonry : Which I call mere Nonſenſe, and all that peruſe this will ſay the ſame, when they are convinc'd that this is the whole Thing ; which they ſoon will find out, only by talking out of this Book to ſome that you know to be Maſons ; but not to let them know that you have read it : You may ſay that you was made at ſome Lodge in the Country, and then ſhew them the Signs and Gripes, and the Words thereunto belonging ; all which are fully deſcrib'd in this Book : Then he will ſoon own you for one of the Fraternity, and take you to his Lodge, as they did me.

Maſ. Have you got that due Guard, or Sign, of an enter'd Apprentice ?

N. B. He draws his Right-hand a-croſs his Throat (as aforeſaid), to ſhew the Maſter that he has.

Maſ. After all this, what was ſaid to you ?

Anſ. I was order'd to be taken back, and veſted with what I had been diveſted of ; and to be brought back to return Thanks, and to receive the Benefit of a Lecture, if Time would permit.

D 2 *Maſ.*

Maf. After you was invefted of what you had been divefted of, what was done to you ?

Anf. I was brought back to the North-weft Corner of the Lodge, in order to return Thanks.

Maf. How did you return Thanks ?

Anf. I ftood in the North-weft Corner of the Lodge, and, with the Inftruction of a Brother, I faid, Mafter, fenior and junior Wardens, fenior and junior Deacons, and the reft of the Brethren of this Lodge, I return you Thanks for the Honour you have done me, in making me a Mafon, and admitting me a Member of this worthy Society.

Maf. What was faid to you then ?

Anf. The Mafter call'd me up to the North-Eaft Corner of the Lodge, or at his Right-hand.

Maf. Did he prefent you with any Thing?

Anf. He prefented me with an Apron, which he put on me ; he told me it was a Badge of Innocency, more antient than the Golden Fleece or the *Roman* Eagle ; more honour'd than the Star and Garter, or any other Order under the Sun, that could be conferr'd upon me at that Time, or any Time hereafter.

Maf. What were the next Things that were fhewn to you ?

Anf. I was fet down by the Mafter's Right-hand and he fhew'd me the working Tools of an enter'd Aprentice.

Maf. What were they ?

Anf. The 24 Inch Gauge, the Square and common Gavel, or fetting Maul.

Maf.

(21)

Maſ. What are their Uſes?

Anſ. The Square to ſquare my Work, the 24 Inch Gauge to meaſure my Work, the common Gavel to knock off all ſuperfluous Matters, whereby the Square may ſet eaſy and juſt.

Maſ. Brother, as we are not all working Maſons, we apply them to our Morals, which we call ſpiritualizing; explain them.

Anſ. The 24 Inch Gauge repreſents the 24 Hours of the Day.

Maſ. How do you ſpend them Brother?

Anſ Six Hours to work in, Six Hours to ſerve God, and Six to ſerve a Friend or a Brother, as far as lies in my Power, without being detrimental to myſelf or Family : and Six Hours to Sleep in.

N. B. This is all the enter'd Apprentice's Lecture, which gives the full Deſcription of his making, and is enough for an Apprentice to learn to get Admittance into a Lodge; but there are ſome fooliſh Reaſons why a Man ſhould be ſerv'd ſo, which I ſhall ſhew you hereafter. But methinks I hear ſome ſay, I am ſurpriz'd that Gentlemen of good Senſe and Reaſon would ſuffer themſelves to be us'd ſo; to be robb'd of all their Money, and all Manner of Metal, and almoſt ſtrip'd naked, and blinded, with a Halter about his Neck! ſo ſay, I. But the Reaſon is, no Man ever was made a Maſon, but has ſome Friends there that were Maſons already, and perhaps under ſome Obligation, who will ſay, we were ſerv'd ſo before, and were not afraid, but you will hear the

Reaſon

(22)

Reafon for it all, then you will be fatisfied, and fay our Meaning is good. I myfelf have feen feveral that would not go through it, 'till their Friends have preached the aforefaid Doctrine. I know feveral that have receiv'd the the firft Step, and would go no farther; for there was one Mr. *T----s*, a Clergyman, and Curate, of St. *Mary Over*'s, in *Southwark*, fo angry and furpriz'd, that he would have been glad to have made his Efcape from them, provided it had been in his Power; but they would not permit him 'till he had received the Apprentice's Obligations, which they call the firft Pill, that you fhant difcover what you have feen; but when he got away, he never came near them more, and thought himfelf very ill us'd. Two or three more were furpriz'd in that Manner at the fame Lodge, *viz.* at Number II. held then at *T----s,* at the Mitre on the *Broad Wall, Chrift Church* in *Surry*, and feveral other Lodges that I have heard of, but this I know to be fact. Alfo the Mafter of a Lodge, who had made a great many Fools, by getting One Pound Five Shillings from each of them: There was half the Money fpent, and the other half kept in the Box for Charitable Ufes; but when they had got to the amount of many Pounds, the Mafter in the Chair, who is fworn moft wickedly not to rob the Lodge, but to ferve it, which he did by carrying it all off, and faid he wanted Charity, therefore he would keep it, and they might do their worft and be d--n'd; and feveral more that I have known to do fuch Tricks, but I

don't

(23)

don't care to mention their **Names,** having faid enough to be underftood. I think the above Number confirms the Character; before they would ferve a Brother, they would rob him, or take away his Character, whereby he may lofe his Bufinefs. I could tell you a great many bad Things they have done one to another, although they are fworn fo bitterly to the contrary: But it would fwell my Pamphlet into a large Volume: Therefore I fhall fay no more, becaufe I would not be too fevere; tho I have faid enough to difplay their Villainy, which I hope will be a Caution to all others.

I fhall now proceed to the Apprentices Reafons, as I promis'd you.

T H E

Enter'd Apprentice's REASONS.

Maf. **W**HY was you neither naked nor cloath'd, bare-foot nor fhod, with a Cable-tow (or Halter) about your Neck?

Anf. If I had recanted, and ran out in the Street, the People would have faid I was mad; but if a Brother had feen me, he would have brought me back, and feen me done Juftice by.

N. B. What a foolifh Reafon is this, for Men of Underftanding to difpute about!

Maf.

Maſ. Why was you hoodwink'd ?

Anſ. That my Heart might conceal, before my Eyes did diſcover ?

Maſ. The ſecond Reaſon, Brother ?

Anſ. As I was in Darkneſs at that Time, I ſhould keep all the World in Darkneſs.

Maſ. Why was you depriv'd of all Metal.

Anſ. That I ſhould bring nothing offenſive, or defenſive into the Lodge.

Maſ. Give me the third Reaſon, Brother ?

Anſ. As I was poor and pennyleſs when I was made a Maſon, it inform'd me that I ſhould aſſiſt all poor and pennyleſs Brethren, as far as lay in my Power.

Maſ. Brother, you told me you gave Three diſtinct Knocks at the Door : Pray what do they ſignify ?

Anſ. A certain text in Scripture.

Maſ. What is that Text, Brother ?

Anſ. Aſk, and you ſhall have ; ſeek, and you ſhall find ; knock, and it ſhall be opened unto you.

Maſ. How do you apply this Text in Maſonry ?

Anſ. I ſought in my Mind ; I aſk'd of my Friend ; I knock'd, and the Door of Maſonry became open unto me.

Maſ. Why had you a Sword, Spear, or ſome other warlike Inſtrument, preſented to your naked Left-breaſt particularly ?

Anſ. Becauſe the Left-breaſt is the neareſt the Heart, that it might be the more a Prick

to

(25)

to my Confcience as it prick'd my flefh at that Time.

Maf. Why was you led three Times round the Lodge ?

Anf. That all the Brethren might fee I was duly prepar'd.

Maf. When you was made an Apprentice, why was your Left-knee bare bent.

Anf. Becaufe the Left-knee is the weakeft Part of my Body, and an enter'd Apprentice is the weakeft Part of Mafonry, which I was then entering into.

N. B. There are fome more Reafons, but they are fo foolifh that they are not worth mentioning; fo I fhall proceed to the Form of the Lodge, as follows.

The Form of a L O D G E.

Maf. BROTHER, we have been talking a great while about a Lodge; Pray what makes a Lodge ?

Anf. A certain Number of Mafons met to-gether to work.

Maf. Pray what Number makes a Lodge ?

Anf. Three, Five, Seven, or Eleven.

Maf. Why do Three make a Lodge, Bro-ther ?

Anf. Becaufe there were three Grand Ma-fons in the building of the World, and alfo

E

that

that noble Piece of Architecture Man ; which are so complete in Proportion, that the Antients began their Architecture by the same Rules.

Maf. The second Reason, Brother ?

Anf. There were three Grand Masons at the building of *Solomon*'s Temple.

Maf. Why do Five make a Lodge ?

Anf. Because every Man is endued with Five Senses.

Maf, What are the Five Senses ?

Anf. Hearing, Seeing, Smelling, Tasting, aad Feeling.

Maf. What Use are those Five Senses to you, in Masonry ?

Anf. Three are of great Use to me, *viz.* Hearing, Seeing, and Feeling.

Maf. What Use are they, Brother ?

Anf. Hearing, is to hear the Word; Seeing, is to see the Sign ; Feeling, is to feel the Gripe ; that I may know a Brother, as well in the Dark as in the Light.

Maf. Why should Seven make a Lodge ?

Anf. Because there are Seven liberal Sciences.

Maf. Will you name them, Brother ?

Anf. Grammar, Rhetoric, Logic, Arithmetic, Geometry, Music, and Astronomy.

Maf. What do those Sciences teach you ?

Anf. Grammar teaches me the Art of writing and speaking the Language, wherein I learn according to the First, Second, and Third Concord.

Maf.

(27)

Maſ. What doth Rhetoric teach you?

Anſ. The Art of ſpeaking and diſcourſing upon any Topic whatſoever.

Maſ. What doth Logic teach you?

Anſ. The Art of reaſoning well, whereby you may find out Truth from Falſhood.

Maſ. What doth Arithmetic teach you?

Anſ. The Virtue of Numbers.

Maſ. What doth Geometry teach you?

Anſ. The Art of meaſuring, whereby the *Egyptians* found out their own Land, or the ſame Quantity which they had before the overflowing of the River *Nile*, which frequently us'd to flow to water their Country; at which Time they fled to the Mountains till it went off again, which made them have continual Quarrels about their Lands; for every Man thought he was robb'd, and had not his Right, till *Euclid* found out Geometry, and meaſur'd every Man his Due, and gave them Plans of each Man's Ground, with the juſt Quantity that belong'd to him; then they were all ſatisfied; and the ſame Rule is continu'd in all Nations to this Day.

Maſ. What doth Muſic teach you, Brother?

Anſ. The Virtue of Sounds.

Maſ. What doth Aſtronomy teach you?

Anſ. The Knowledge of the heavenly Bodies.

N. B. See *Brandt's* Aſtronomical Tables, and you will have a full Deſcription of the laſt Science. But I believe you may content yourſelf without any other Authors upon

E 2   this

(28)

this Head, for I go as far as any of the Free Mafons do in their Lectures, and rather further, which I am obliged to do to make it plain, that it may be underftood to the meaneft Capacity. That which is not in the Lecture is marked thus, *N. B.*

Maf. Why fhould Eleven make a Lodge, Brother ?

Anf. There were Eleven *Patriarcbs*, when *Jofepb* was fold into *Egypt*, and fuppos'd to be loft.

Maf. The Second Reafon, Brother ?

Anf. There were but Eleven Apoftles when *Judas* had betray'd Chrift.

Maf. What Form is your Lodge ?

Anf. An Oblong Square.

Maf. How long, Brother ?

Anf. From Eaft to Weft.

Maf. How wide, Brother ?

Anf. Between North and South.

Maf. How high, Brother ?

Anf. From the Earth to the Heavens.

Maf. How deep, Brother ?

Anf. From the Surface of the Earth to the Center,

Maf. Why is your Lodge faid to be from the Surface to the Center of the Earth ?

Anf. Becaufe that Mafonry is Univerfal.

Maf. Why is your Lodge fituated Eaft and Weft ?

Anf. Becaufe all Churches and Chapels are, or ought to be fo,.

Maf.

(29)

Maſ. Why ſo, Brother ?

Anſ. Becauſe the Goſpel was firſt preached in the Eaſt, and extended itſelf to the Weſt.

Maſ. What ſupports your Lodge ?

Anſ. Three great Pillars.

Maſ. What are their Names ?

Anſ. Wiſdom, Strength and Beauty.

Maſ. Who doth the Pillar of Wiſdom repreſent ?

Anſ. The Maſter in the Eaſt.

Maſ. Who doth the Pillar of Strength repreſent ?

Anſ. The Senior Warden in the Weſt.

Maſ. Who doth the Pillar of Beauty repreſent ?

Anſ. The Junior Warden in the South.

Maſ. Why ſhould the Maſter repreſent the Pillar of Wiſdom ?

Anſ. Becauſe he gives Inſtructions to the Crafts to carry on their Work in a proper Manner, with good Harmony.

Maſ. Why ſhould the Senior Warden repreſent the Pillar of Strength ?

Anſ. As the Sun ſets to finiſh the Day, ſo the Senior Warden ſtands in the Weſt to pay the Hirelings their Wages ; which is the Strength and Support of all Buſineſs.

Maſ. Why ſhould the Junior Warden repreſent the Pillar of Beauty ?

Anſ. Becauſe he ſtands in the South, at high Twelve at Noon, which is the Beauty of the Day, to call the Men off from Work to Refreſhment, and to ſee that they come on again

in

(30)

in due Time, that the Mafter may have Pleafure and Profit therein.

Maf. Why is it faid that your Lodge is
fupported by thefe Three great Pillars, Wifdom, Strength and Beauty?

Anf. Becaufe Wifdom, Strength and Beauty is the Finifher of all Works, and nothing
can be carried on without them.

Maf. Why fo, Brother?

Anf. Becaufe there is Wifdom to contrive,
Strength to fupport, and Beauty to adorn.

Maf. Had you any Covering to your
Lodge?

Anf. Yes, a cloudy Canopy, of divers Colours, or the Clouds.

Maf. How blows a Mafon's Wind, Brother?

Anf. Due Eaft and Weft.

Maf. What is it o' Clock, Brother?
Anf. High Twelve.

Maf. Call the Men off from Work to Refrefhment, and fee that they come on again in
due Time.

[*The End of the enter'd Apprentice's Lecture.*]

The

(3**1**)

The enter'd Apprentice's Song, which is sung after grave Business is done, or after making a Brother.

I.

C O M E let us prepare,
　　We *Brothers* that are,
Assembled on merry Occasion ;
　　Let's drink, laugh, and sing ;
　　Our Wine has a Spring ;
Here's a Health to an *Accepted Mason*.

II.

　　The World is in pain
　　Our *Secrets* to gain,
And still let them wonder and gaze on ;
　　They ne'er can divine
　　The *Word* or the *Sign*
Of a *Free* and *Accepted Mason*.

III.

　　'Tis *This*, and 'tis *That*,
　　They cannot tell *What*,
Why so many *Great Men* of the Nation
　　Should *Aprons* put on,
　　To make themselves one
With a *Free* and an *Accepted Mason*.

IV.

　　Great *Kings*, *Dukes* and *Lords*,
　　Have laid by their Swords,
Our *Myst'ry* to put a good Grace on,
　　And ne'er been asham'd
　　To hear themselves nam'd
With a *Free* and an *Accepted Mason*.

V. An-

32

V.

Antiquity's Pride
We have on our Side,
And it maketh Men juft in their Station :
There's nought but what's Good,
To be underftood
By a *Free* and an *Accepted Mafon.*

VI.

We're true and fincere,
And juft to the *Fair*,
Who will truft us on ev'ry Occafion ;
No Mortals can more
The *Ladies* adore,
Than a *Free* and an *Accepted Mafon.*

VII.

Then join *Hand* in *Hand*,
T' each other firm ftand,
Let's be merry, and put a bright Face on :
What Mortal can boaft
So *Noble a Toaft*,
As a *Free* and an *Accepted Mafon.*

VIII.

W'ere true and fincere,
And juft to the *Fair*,
Who will truft us on ev'ry Occafion ;
No Mortal can more,
The Ladies adore,
Than a *Free* and an *Accepted Mafon.*

N. B. When they fing the aforefaid Song,
they all ftand round a great Table, and join
Hands a-crofs, that is, your Right-hand takes
hold

(33)

hold of your Left-hand Man's Left-hand; and your Left-hand Man, with his Right-hand, takes hold of his left Man's Left-hand, and so crossing all round. But when they say the last Verse, they jump up all together, ready to shake the Floor down: I myself have been below, where there has been a Lodge, and have heard the People say, L—d d---mn their Bloods, what are they doing? They will shake the Place down, I'll stay here no longer. This they call driving of Piles, to amuse the world; but they shall not be amus'd any longer, but shall know every particular, and the foolish Reasons they give for them.

How they call off the Men from Work to Refreshment.

THE Master whispers to the senior Deacon at his Right-hand, and says, 'tis my Will and Pleasure that this Lodge is called off from Work to Refreshment during Pleasure; then the senior Deacon carries it to the junior Warden, and whispers the same Words in his Ear, and he whispers it in the Ear of the junior Deacon at his Right-hand, and he carries it to the junior Warden, and whispers the same to him, who declares it with a loud Voice, and says, it is our Master's Will and Pleasure, that this Lodge is called from Work to Refreshment, during Pleasure; then he sets up his Column, and the Senior lays his down; for the

F   Care

(34)

Care of the Lodge is in the Hands of the junior Warden, while they are at Refreſhment.

N. B. The ſenior and junior Warden have each
of them a Column in their Hand, about
Twenty Inches long, which repreſents the
Two Columns of the Porch at *Solomon's*
Temple, Boaz and Jachin.*

  The Senior is Boaz, or Strength.
  The Junior is Jachin, or to eſtabliſh.

  * Vide 1 Kings, Chap. vii.

How to call on to Work again.

IT is the ſame as calling off from Work, only with this Difference ; it is our Maſter's
Will and Pleaſure that this Lodge is called off
from Refreſhment to Work; then the Junior
lays down his Column, and the ſenior Warden
ſets up his ; ſo they proceed to a Lecture,
which they call Work.

N. B. If time does not permit for the Craft's
Lecture, as it very ſeldom does, having gone
through the aforeſaid Lecture, then they
cloſe the Lodge ; which is much the ſame
as opening, only with this Difference ; the
ſenior Warden declares it, and ſays,

  It is our Maſter's Will and Pleaſure, that
this Lodge ſtands clos'd till the firſt, or third
Wedneſday in the next Month (or according to
                                                    the

(35)

the Nights that their Lodge is held on), except a Lodge of Emergency, and that you ſhall have timely Notice of ; then they take off their Jewels, and get as drunk as Free-maſons may be ; and ſing and get drunk, and that's all.

The FELLOW-CRAFT's *Part.*

Maſ. BROTHER, are you a Fellow-Craft ?

Anſ. I am ; try me, prove me.

Maſ. Where was you made a Craft ?
Anſ. In a juſt and lawful Lodge of Crafts.

Maſ. How was you prepar'd to be made a Craft ?
Anſ. I was neither naked not cloath'd, bare-foot nor ſhod ; in a halting moving Poſture, depriv'd of all Metal, I was led to the Door of he Lodge by the Hand of a Brother.

Maſ. How got you admittance ?
Anſ. By Three diſtinct Knocks.

Maſ. What was ſaid to you within ?
Anſ. Who comes there.

Maſ. Your Anſwer, Brother?
Anſ. One who hath ſerv'd his Time juſtly and lawfully as an enter'd Apprentice, and now begs to become more perfect in Maſonry, by being admitted a Fellow-Craft.

F 2   *Maſ.*

(36)

Maſ. How do you expect to attain it ?

Anſ. By the Benefit of a Paſs-word:

Maſ. Have you got that Paſs-word ?

Anſ. I have.

Maſ. Give it me ?

Anſ. SHIBBOLETH.*

Maſ. What did he ſay to you then ?

Anſ. Paſs, Shibboleth.

Maſ. What became of you then ?

Anſ. I was led twice round the Lodge.

Maſ. Where did you meet with the firſt Oppoſition ?

Anſ. At the Back of the ſenior Warden, where I made the ſame Repetition as at the Door.

Maſ. Where did you meet with the ſecond Oppoſition ?

Anſ. At the Back of the Maſter, where I made the ſame Repetition as at the Door.

Maſ. What did he do with you ?

Anſ. He order'd me back to the ſenior Warden, to receive Inſtruction.

Maſ. What Inſtructions did he give you ?

Anſ. He taught me to ſhew the Maſter my due Guard, and to take Two Steps upon the ſecond Step of a right-angl'd oblong Square, with my Right-knee bent bare, my Left-foot forming a Square, my Body upright, my Right-hand upon the holy Bible, my Left-arm ſupported by the Point of the Compaſſes, forming a Square ; where I took tht Obligation of a Fellow-Craft.

* Vide Judges, Chap. xii.

Maſ.

41

(**37**)

Maſ. Have you got that Obligation, Brother?

Anſ. I have, Worſhipful.

Maſ. Will you repeat it, Brother ?

Anſ. I'll do my Endeavour, with your Aſſiſt nce, Worſhipful.

Maſ. Stand up and begin.

Anſ.   I *W*----- *V*------,

Of my own Will and Accord, and in the Preſence of Almighty God and this right worſhipful Lodge, dedicated to St. *John*, do hereby,
and hereon, moſt ſolemnly and ſincerely ſwear,
that I will always hail, conceal, and never will
reveal that Part of a Fellow-Craft to an enter'd
Apprentice, or either of them, except it be in
a true and lawful Lodge of Crafts, him or
them, whom I ſhall find to be ſuch after juſt
Trial and due Examination.

I furthermore do ſwear, that I will anſwer all
Signs and Summonſes ſent to me from a Lodge
of Crafts, within the Length of my Cable-Tow.

I alſo ſwear, that I will not wrong a Brother,
or ſee him wrong'd, but give him timely Notice of all approaching Dangers whatſoever, as
far as my Knowledge leads me. I will alſo ſerve
a Brother as far as lies in my Power, without
being detrimental to myſelf or Family ; and I
will keep all my Brother's Secrets as my own,
that ſhall be delivered to me as ſuch, Murder
and Treaſon only excepted.

And that at my own free Will, all this I
ſwear, with a firm and ſteady Reſolution to
perform the ſame, without any Equivocation

or

or Hefitation in me whatfoever, under no lefs
Penalty than to have my Heart torn from un-
der my naked Left-breaft, and given to the
Vultures of the Air as a Prey: So help me
God, and keep me ftedfaft in this my Craft's
Obligation.

[*He kiffes the Book.*]

N. B. The Length of the Cable-Tow is
Three Miles ; therefore if a Brother is Three
Miles from his Lodge, he is clear of all Fines,
and of this Obligation ; for it faith within the
Length of my Cable-Tow.

Maf. After you receiv'd this Obligation,
what was fhewn to you ?
Anf. The Sign of a Fellow-Craft.

N. B. This Sign is by putting your Right-
hand to your Left-breaft, and keeping your
Thumb fquare, and your Left-hand upright,
forming a Square.

Maf. What was next done to you ?
Anf. He took me by the Right-hand and
gave me the Gripe and Word of a Fellow-
Craft and Pafs-Gripe.

N. B. The Pafs-Gripe is by putting your
Thumb-nail between the firft and fecond
Joint of the Right-hand, and the Word is
Shibboleth. The Craft's Gripe is on the fe-
cond Joint of the aforefaid Hand, and the
Word is *Jachin.*

Maf. What did he then do to you ?
Anf. He took me by the Right-hand, and
faid, rife up Brother *Jachin.*

Maf.

(39)

Maſ. What did he do then to you?

Anſ. He order'd me back, and to be inveſted of what I had been diveſted of, and brought back in order to return Thanks.

N. B. He returns Thanks in the ſame Manner as the Apprentice, only with this Difference, for admitting a Fellow-Craft.

Maſ. After you was thus admitted a Fellow-Craft, did you ever work as a Craft?

Anſ. Yes in the Building of the Temple.

Maſ. Where did you receive your Wages?

Anſ. In the Middle Chamber.

Maſ. When you came to the Door of the Middle Chamber, who did you ſee?

Anſ. A Warden.

Maſ. What did he demand of you?

Anſ. The Paſs-word of a Craft.

Maſ. did you give it him?

Anſ. I did.

Maſ. What is it?

Anſ. SHIBBOLETH.

Maſ. How got you to the Middle Chamber?

Anſ. Through the Porch.

Maſ. Did you ſee any Thing worth your Notice?

Anſ. I did.

Maſ. What was it?

Anſ. Two fine Braſs Pillars.

Maſ. What were they call'd?

Anſ. BOAZ and JACHIN.

Maſ.

(40)

Maſ. How high were theſe Pillars ?

Anſ. Thirty-five Cubits, with a Chapiter Five Cubits, which makes it Forty high.*

N. B. In the firſt of *Kings*, Chap. vii. Ver. 20, it ſays, They were but 18 Cubits high, and a Line of 12 Cubits meaſured them round, that is, about 4 Cubits Diameter, which is greatly out of Proportion according to all Orders that ever were or ever will be ; as any muſt ſay, that underſtands Architecture, for it is not quite four Diameters and an half, which is too ſhort by four Diameters at leaſt ; for if they were in the *Dorick* Order, they ſhould be eight Diameters. Therefore, how thick and clumſy they muſt look, to be but half the Height they ſhould be, or a little better. As for Example, ſuppoſe the Monument upon *Fiſh-ſtreet-hill*, which is after the *Dorick* Order, was but half the Height, and the ſame Diameter, how would it look ? very thick and clumſy, like as it were all of a Lump.

But this can't be the Thing with theſe two Columns, for it is plain that *Solomon*'s Temple was a grand Building, and every Thing in Proportion, and it anſwers exactly with the *Corinthian* or Compoſite Order, for it is ten Diameters high, or thereabouts ; and it is ſaid in Chap. iii. Ver. 15, of the Second Book of *Chronicles*, 35 Cubits high, and the Chapiters 5 Cubits each, which makes 40 Cubits ; the Diameter 4 Cubits, and the aforeſaid Order is 10 Diameters high, that is, 4 Times is 40, which

* Vide 2 Chron. Chap. iii. Ver. 15.

(41)

which is juft 60 Feet high of our *Englifh* Meafure*.

Ma What were they adorned with Brother?·
Anf. Two Chapiters, Five Cubits high each.

Maf. What elfe were they adorned with?
Anf. Net-work, Lillywork and Pomegra-nates.

Maf. Were they hollow, Brother?
Anf. They were hollow.

Maf. How thick was the Rhind or Shell?
Anf. Four Inches, or a Hand's Breadth.

Maf. Where were they caft?
Anf. On the Plain of *Jordan*, in Clay Ground, between *Succoth* and *Zartha*, where the reft of *Solomon*'s holy Veffels were caft.

Maf. Who caft them?
Anf. Hiram Abiff, the Widow's Son.

N. B. Some Mafters of Lodges will argue up-on Reafons about the holy Veffels in the Tem-ple, and the Windows and Doors, the Length, Breadth and Height of every Thing in the Temple. Saying, why was it fo and fo? One will give one Reafon, and another will give another Reafon, and thus they will continue for two or three Hours in this Part and the Maf-ter-Part; but this happens but very feldom, except an *Irifhman* fhould come, who likes to hear himfelf talk, afking, why were they round?

G   Why

* There are Three Sorts of Cubits, viz. the King's Cubit, Three Feet Englifh Meafure; the holy Cubit, One Foot Six Inches; the common Cubit, One Foot Nine Inches: Therefore, whenever you read of the Word Cubit in the Bible, it is One Foot Six Inches.

(42)

Why were they fquare ? Why were they hollow ? Why were the Stones coftly ? Why
were they hewn Stones and faw'd Stones, &c.
fome give one Reafon and fome give another ;
thus you fee that every Man's Reafon is not
alike. Therefore, if I give you my Reafon, it
may not be like another ; but any Man that
reads the foregoing and following Work, and
confults the 5th, 6th, 7th and 8th Chapters of
the firft Book of *Kings*, and the 2d, 3d and 4th
of the fecond Book of *Chronicles*, may reafon
as well as the beft of them ; for I have laid all
the Rules down plain to go by.

[*The End of the Fellow-Crafts Part.*]

XXXXXXXXXXXXXXXXXXXXXXXX

The FELLOW-CRAFTS Song.

I.

HAIL Masonry ? Thou *Craft* divine ?
　　Glory of Earth, from Heaven reveal'd ;
Which do'ft with Jewels precious fhine,
　　From all but Mafons Eyes conceal'd.

CHORUS.

Thy Praifes due who can rehearfe,
In nervous Profe, or flowing Verfe.

II.

As Men from Brutes diftinguifh'd are,
　　A *Mafon* other Men excels ;
For what's in Knowledge choice and rare
　　But in his Breaft fecurely dwells ?

CHORUS.

(43)

CHORUS.

His silent Breast and faithful Heart
Preserves the Secrets of the Art.

III.

From scorching Heat, and piercing Cold;
   From Beasts, whose Roar the Forest rends;
From the Assaults of Warriors bold
   The Masons Art Mankind defends.

CHORUS.

Be to this Art due Honour paid,
From which Mankind receives such Aid.

IV.

Ensigns of State, that feed our Pride,
   Distinctions troublesome and vain!
By *Masons* true are laid aside:
   Arts free-born *Sons* such Toys disdain;

CHORUS.

Ennobled by the Name *they bear,*
Distinguish'd by the Badge *they wear.*

V.

Sweet Fellowship, from Envy free:
   Friendly Converse of Brotherhood;
The *Lodge*'s lasting Cement be!
   Which has for Ages firmly stood.

CHORUS.

A Lodge, *thus built for Ages past.*
Has lasted, and will ever last.

G 2   VI. Then

(44)

VI.

Then in our Songs be Juſtice done
   To thoſe who have enrich'd the *Art*,
From *Jabal* down to *Burlington*,
   And let each Brother bear a Part.

C H O R U S.

Let noble Maſons *Healths go round*;
Their Praiſe in lofty Lodge *reſound*.

N. B. The Fellow-Craft's Clap is by forming the Craft's Sign, *i. e.* by holding your
Left-hand up, keeping it ſquare ; then clap
with your Right-hand and Left together, and
from thence ſtrike your Left-Breaſt with your
Right-hand ; then ſtrike your Apron, and
your Right-foot going at the ſame Time.
This is done altogether as one Clap, or at leaſt
ſhould be, which makes a great Shaking on
the Floor, and what they call driving of Piles
to amuſe the World; but they ſhall not be a-
muſed any longer, but ſhall have the Truth.
Nay, I have known ſome Lodges that have
had Shores ſet below to ſupport the Floor,
while they have been at work as they call it.

How

(45)

How to difcover a Mafon by drinking with him in Company, and what Degree of Mafonry he has paft, and none of the Company can difcover it but Mafons.

IF he takes his Pot or Glafs, and draws it a-crofs his Throat before he drinks or after, then he is an Apprentice, becaufe that is the Penalty of his Obligation: that he would have his Throat cut a-crofs before he would difcover any thing of Mafonry.

Or, if he draws it a-crofs his Left-breaft, touching the fame, he is a Craft, for that is the Penalty of the Craft's Obligation, *i. e.* He would fooner have his Heart torn from under his naked Left-breaft, and given to the Vul-tures of the Air as a Prey, than difcover any Part of Mafonry.

Or, if he draws it a-crofs his Belly, he is a Mafter, for that is the Penalty of the Mafter's Obligation; *i. e.* He would fooner have his Body fever'd in two; one Part carried to the South and the other to the North, his Bowels burnt to Afhes in the South, than he would difcover any Part of Mafonry.

N. B. He may do the fame with his naked Right-hand as with a Pot or Glafs, but it is lefs taken notice of with a Pot or Glafs than with your Hand.

But in the Lodge they always drink out of Glaffes, and put them down as it is faid in the Apprentices Part; but if it is a Lodge of all Mafter Mafons, before they fet the Glafs down upon the Table where they all fit round, as

afore-

(46)

aforefaid, they draw it a-crofs their Throat,
from thence a-crofs their Left-breaft, touching the fame, from thence a-crofs their Belly,
and then making three Motions to fet it down,
at the Third fet it down altogether; the
Mafter gives the Word, faying, Here goes one,
two and three, fetting it down; but if it is a
Craft's Lodge, they draw it twice a-crofs their
Throats and once to their Breaft; and if it is
an Apprentice's Lodge, they draw it three
Times a-crofs their Throats, and fets it down
at the third Motion, as aforefaid.

Thus they will many Times continue exer-
cifing till Morning, though their Family want
them at home. Come, they will fay, let us
have the other Fire, then we will go! Says a-
nother, we can't, for our Bowl is out! Then
fays another, let's have it fill'd again! This
has been the Ruin of Mafonry, which was far
from the firft Defign of it; but Liquor
makes Men forget that they are Men, and
makes all good things become corrupted and
bad.

Cura fugit multo diluiturque mero
Tunc Dolor & Curæ rugaque Frontis abeft.

Full Bowls, or chafe, or elfe diffolve our Cares, ⎫
Then far away are banifh'd Griefs and Fears, ⎬
Nor thoughtful Wrinkle in the Face appears. ⎭

Thus, a great many People think that it is a
great Service for a Man to be made a Mafon;
fo it is, to be his Ruin; and when he is in the
greateft Diftrefs they will talk againft him, becaufe he can't pay what they demand. I can't
fay that I ever knew any Mafon of late Years,
get

51

(47)

get any Thing by going to Lodges, without it is a Publican that keeps the Houfe. Although they are fworn to ferve a Brother, I never knew they did, but hurt him. I have known Mafons to arreft a Brother, fummon a Brother to the Court of Requeft, and feize a Brother's Goods, for lefs than Twenty Shillings. I have likewife known them put a Brother In Goal, and do him a great deal more Mifchief, which I don't care to fpeak too plain to their Confci-ences, which I am in hopes to foften ; for when it has been in their power to ferve a Brother, they have, at the fame Time, endeavoured to ruin him. Therefore, I hope this will be a Warning to all honeft Men to keep from thefe Oaths, without they intend to perform them, for they are very folemn.

I think I have heard fome fay, it is furpriz-ing that they all fhould be bad ! No, God forbid they fhould, but I will tell you the Reafon why they are fo.

There are a great many good Men, Mem-bers of Lodges, that little think of the Vil-lainy that is carried on among fome of them ; but when he finds them out, he'll leave the Lodge, and be no more concerned with them, but he will not tell his Reafons to the World ; if he did, he would be forfworn. I have known fome young Brethren to have found them out a little after they were made, and have left the Lodge upon that Account. This is the Reafon that they act fo contrary to their Obligation, becaufe honeft Men can't bear it long, fo the Scum of the Earth are left to be Mafters of Lodges.

The

(4⁸)

✻✻✻✻✻✻✻✻✻✻✻✻✻✻✻✻✻✻✻✻✻✻✻✻

The M A S T E R's Part.

Maſ. WHERE have you been, Brother ?
       Anſ. I have been to the Weſt,

Maſ. And where are you going ?
Anſ. To the Eaſt,

Maſ. What makes you leave the Weſt and go to the Eaſt ?
Anſ. Becauſe the Light of the Goſpel was firſt ſhewn in the Eaſt.

Maſ. What are you going to do in the Eaſt, Brother ?
Anſ. To ſeek for a Lodge of Maſters.

Maſ. Then I preſume you are a Maſter Maſon, Brother ?
Anſ. I am ſo taken amongſt Maſters.

Maſ. Where was you paſt Maſter ?
Anſ. In a Lodge of Maſters.

Maſ. How was you prepar'd to be made a Maſter ?
Anſ. I had my Shoes taken from off my Feet, both my Arms and Breaſt naked, depriv'd of all Metal. I was led to the Door of the Lodge.

N. B. In the Craft's Part, the Right-breaſt is naked, and the Right-ſhoe off, and in. the Apprentices Part, the Left-arm and Left-breaſt is naked, with the Left-ſhoe off, and the Maſter's Part, as aforeſaid in the Lecture.

Maſ.

(49)

Maſ. How got you Admittance ?

Anſ. By Three diſtinct Knocks.

Maſ. What was ſaid to you then within ?

Anſ. Who comes there ?

Maſ. Your Anſwer, Brother ?

Anſ. One who hath juſtly and lawfully ſerved his Time as an Enter'd Apprentice, and ſome Time Fellow-Craft, now begs to become more perfect in Maſonry to be made a Maſter.

Maſ. How do you expect to attain it ?

Anſ. By the Benefit of a Paſs-word.

Maſ. Will you give me that Paſs-word ?

Anſ. I will.

Maſ. Give it me then.

Anſ. TUBAL-CAIN.

Maſ. What was ſaid to you then ?

Anſ. Enter TUBAL-CAIN.

Maſ. How was you diſpos'd of ?

Anſ. I was led once round the Lodge.

Maſ. Where did you meet with the firſt Oppoſition ?

Anſ. At the Back of the Maſter.

Maſ. What did he demand of you ?

Anſ. The ſame as at the Door.

Maſ. How did he diſpoſe of you ?

Anſ. He order'd me back to the ſenior Warden in the Weſt to receive Inſtructions.

Maſ. What were the Inſtructions you received of the ſenior Warden ?

Anſ. He taught me as I ſtood in the Weſt to ſhew the Maſter in the Eaſt my due Guard or Sign of an Apprentice, and to take one

H   Step

Step upon the First Step of the Right-Angle Oblong Square, my other Foot forming a Square.

Secondly, I was taught to take two Steps upon the same Oblong Square, shewing him the Sign of a Fellow-Craft.

Thirdly, I was taught to take Three Steps upon the same Oblong Square, with both my Knees bent bare, my Body upright, my Right-hand upon the Holy Bible, both the Points of the Compasses extended to my Right and Left-breast, where I took that solemn Obligation or Oath of a Master Mason.

Maf. Can you repeat the Obligation you speak of?

Anf. I'll do my Endeavour, Worshipful, with your Assistance.

Maf. Stand up and begin, Brother.

Anf.   I. W——— V———,

Of my own free Will and Accord, and in the Presence of Almighty God, and this right worshipful Lodge, dedicated to St. *John*, do hereby and hereon most solemnly and sincerely swear, that I will always hail, conceal, and never will reveal, that Part of a Master Mason to a Fellow-Craft, no more than that of a Fellow Craft to an enter'd Apprentice, or any of them to the rest of the World, except it be to a true and lawful Lodge of Masters, him, or them, whom I shall find to be such, after just Trial and due Examination.

                      I further-

(51)

I furthermore do fwear, that I will anfwer all Signs and Summonfes, fent to me from a Lodge of Mafters, within the length of my Cable-tow.

I alfo will keep all my Brother's Secrets as my own, that is delivered to me as fuch, Murder and Treafon only excepted, and that at my own free Will : I will not wrong a Brother or fee him wrong'd, but give him timely Notice of all approaching Dangers, as far as my Knowledge leads me.

I alfo will ferve a Brother as far as lies in my Power, without being detrimental to my-felf or Family.

And I furthermore do promife, that I will not have any carnal Converfation with a Bro-ther's Wife, Sifter or Daughter, and that I will never difcover what is done in the Lodge, but that I will be agreeable to all Laws what-foever. All this I fwear, with a firm and fteady Refolution to perform the fame, with-out any Hefitation in me whatfoever, under no lefs Penalty than to have my Body fever'd in two, the one Part carried to the South, and the other to the North ; my Bowels burnt to Afhes in the South, and the Afhes to be fcatter'd before the Four Winds, that fuch a vile Wretch as I fhould be remember'd no more amongft any Manner of Men, (particu-larly Mafons) fo help me God, and keep me ftedfaft in this my Mafter's Obligation.

[*He kiffes the Book.*]

Maf. What was fhewnto you after you had received this Obligation?

H 2   *Anf.*

(52)

Anf. One of the Mafter's Signs.

N. B. It is by drawing your Right-hand edgeways acrofs your Belly, which is the Penalty of your Mafter's Obligation. He
takes you then by the Apprentices Gripe,
and fays, what's this ? You fay the Gripe
of an enter'd Apprentice.

Maf. Has it got a Name ?
Anf. It has.

Maf. Will you give it me ?
Anf. BOAZ.

Maf. Will you be of or from ?
Anf. From.

Maf. From what, Brother ?
Anf. From an enter'd Apprentice to a Fellow-Craft.

Maf. Pafs Brother.

N. B. Then he puts his Thumb between the
Firft and Second Joint, which is the Pafs
Gripe, and you fay SHIBBOLETH.

Maf. What was done to you then ?
Anf. He took me by the Gripe of a Fellow-
Craft, and faid what is this ?

Maf. Your Anfwer, Brother ?
Anf. The Gripe of a Fellow-Craft.

Maf. Has it got a Name ?
Anf. It has.

Maf. Will you give it me ?
Anf. JACHIN.

Maf. What was faid to you then ?

Anf.

(53)

Anf. Rife up Brother JACHIN, Obligated Mafter.

Maf. What was faid to you then, Brother?
Anf. He told me I then reprefented one of the greateft Men in the World, our grand Mafter *Hiram*, who was killed juft at the Finifhing of the firft Temple, as you fhall hear.

There were Fifteen Fellow-Crafts, finding the Temple almoft finifhed, and they had not received the Mafter's Word, becaufe their Time was not come, therefore they agreed to extort them from their Mafter *Hiram* the firft Opportunity, that they might pafs for Mafters in other Countries, and have Mafter's Wages; but twelve of thefe Crafts recanted, and the other three were refolved to carry it on; their Names were *Jubela*, *Jubelo* and *Jubelum*. Thefe three Crafts knowing it was always the Mafter's Cuftom at high Twelve at Noon, when the Men were call'd off to Refrefhment, to go into *Sanctum Sanctorum*, to pray to the true and living God: Thofe three Ruffians placed themfelves at the three Entrances of the Temple, *viz.* The Weft Door, the South Door and Eaft Door.

There was no Entrance in at the North, becaufe the Sun darts no Rays from thence: Thus they waited while he had made his Prayer to the Lord, to have the Word and Gripe as he came out, or his Life; but fome Mafons fay, as he went in. So *Hiram* came to the Eaft Door, and *Jubela* demanded the Mafter's Word: He told him he did not receive it in
                                    fuch

such a Manner; but he must wait, and Time and a little Patience would bring him to it, for it was not in his Power to deliver it alone, except Three together, *viz. Solomon*, King of *Israel*; *Hiram*, King of *Tyre*; and *Hiram Abiff*. He not being satisfied with this Answer, struck him a-cross the Throat with a 24 Inch Gauge: He fled from thence to the South Door, where he thought to have made his Way; but he was accosted in the same Manner by *Jubelo*, to whom he gave the same Answer as the former; but he not being satisfied, gave him a Blow with the Square upon his Left-breast, which made him reel: But having recover'd his Strength, he fled to the West Door, where he thought to have made his Escape; but he was accosted in the same Manner, as at the two other Doors, by *Jubelum*, to whom he made the same Reply as before; but he not being satisfied therewith, gave him a greater Blow than either of the former, with a common Gavel, or Setting Maul, upon his Head, which prov'd his Death. After this they carry'd him out at the West Door, and hid him in a Heap of Rubbish till high Twelve at Night, when they found Means to bury him on the Side of a Hill, in a handsome Grave, Six Foot East and West, and Six Foot perpendicular.

N. B. Some Masons say that he was not carry'd out at the West Door, but was bury'd in the Place where he was killed.

They hold that the Three Ruffians took up a Stone in the Temple, and made a Hole and put him in, and cover'd him over with the
Stone,

(55)

Soone, and carry'd the Rubbifh out in their Aprons; but which it is I can't fay, nor come at the exact Truth: For fome Mafons fay he was carry'd out, and fome fay not; fo I leave it to them to determine.

Maf. After you was thus knock'd down, what was faid to you then?

Anf. He faid I reprefented one of the great-eft Men in the World, our Grand-Mafter *Hi-ram*, lying dead.

N. B. The junior Warden ftruck you with a 24 Inch Gauge, a-crofs your Throat; the fenior Warden ftruck you with the Square, upon your Left-breaft; and the Mafter ftruck you upon the Head and kill'd you: So you are laid down upon the Floor on your Back, fuppos'd to be dead, tho' you are not hurt; but only to reprefent the Death of your Ma-fter *Hiram*.

The *French* have a very folemn Way of reprefenting his Death; for when you come into the Lodge to be made a Mafter, there is a Brother laid down in the Place where you are to-lie, with his Face all befmear'd with Blood; and they fay to you, Brother don't be frighten-en'd, for one of our Brother's is kill'd becaufe he would not deliver the Mafter's Word and Gripe to the Three Fellow-Crafts, that had no Right to it; and it is the Duty of us all fo to do, to die before we will deliver any Part of Mafonry to them that have no Right to it.

When you kneel down to receive the Obli-gation, the fuppos'd dead Man lies behind you; and while you are reading the Obligati-on

(56)

on and Hiftory of his Death, he gets up unknown to you, and you are laid down in his Place, as afore faid, according to the *Englifh* Method ; and this is all the Difference between the *French* and *Englifh* in their making of Mafons.

Maf. What was faid to you then ?

Anf. As I lay upon my Back, he gave me the whole Account how *Hiram* was found, and of his rifing and taking the Three Ruffians that murder'd him.

Our Mafter *Hiram* being miffing, as he did not come to view the Work as ufual, fo King *Solomon* made great Enquiry after him, and could not hear any Thing of him, therefore he fuppos'd him dead : The Twelve Fellow-Crafts that had recanted, hearing the faid Report, their Confciences pricking them, went and acquainted King *Solomon*, with white Aprons and Gloves, as Badges of their Innocency ; and King *Solomon* fent them in fearch of the Three Ruffians which had abfconded : They divided into Four Parts, Three North, Three South, Three Eaft, and Three Weft : One of thofe Parties travell'd down to the Sea of *Joppa*; one of them fat himfelf down to reft, by the Side of a Rock, he hearing a frightful Lamentation in a Clift of the Rock. Oh ! that I had had my Throat cut a-crofs, and my Tongue torn out by the Root, and that buried in the Sands of the Sea at Low-water Mark, a Cable Length from Shore, where the Tide ebbs and flows in 24 Hours, rather

(57)

rather than I had been concerned in the Death of our Mafter *Hiram*. Says the other; Oh! that I had had my Heart torn from under my naked Left-Breaft, and given to the Vultures of the Air as a Prey, rather than I had been concerned in the Death of fo good a Mafter. But Oh! fays *Jubelum*, I ftruck him more hard than you both, for I killed him; Oh! that I had had my body fevered in two, one Part carried to the South, and the other to the North; my Bowels burnt to Afhes in the South, and the Afhes fcattered before the Four Winds of the Earth, rather than I had been concerned in the Death of our Mafter *Hiram*,

This Brother hearing this forrowful Lamentation, hailed the other Two, and they went into the Clift of the Rock, and took them and bound them, and brought them before King *Solomon*, and they owned what had pafs'd, and what they had done, and did not defire to live; therefore *Solomon* order'd their own Sentences to be laid upon them: Says he, they have fign'd their own Death, and let it be upon them as they have faid.

Jubela was taken out, and his Throat cut a-crofs, &c. *Jubelo*'s Heart was torn from under his naked Left-breaft, &c. *Jubelum*'s Body was fevered in two, and one Part carry'd to the South, and the other to the North, &c.

After this King *Solomon* fent thofe 12 Crafts to raife their Mafter *Hiram*, in order that he might be interred in *Sanctum Sanctorum*. And *Solomon* told them, that if they could not find a Key-word in him or about him, it was loft;

I   for

for there were but Three in the World that knew it, and it can never be deliver'd without we Three are together; but now One is dead, therefore it is loft. But for the future, the firft occafion'd Sign and Word that is fpoke at his raifing, fhall be his ever after. So they went to raife him; and when they had clear'd the Rubbifh, they faw their Mafter lie dead, in a bruifed Condition; for he having already lairi 15 Days, they lifted up both their Hands above their Heads in a great Surprize, and faid, O Lord my God, (which is the grand Sign of a Mafter-Mafon.)

Maf. How was he rais'd, Brother, when they had thus found him lying dead?
Anf. By the Five Points of Fellowfhip.

Maf. What are the Five Points of Fellow-fhip?
Anf. He was taken by the enter'd Apprentice's Gripe, but the Skin is fuppofed to flip off; he was then taken by the Craft's Gripe, and that flipped alfo; then he was taken by a more firm Gripe, that is, their Four Fingers Nails of their Right-hand ftuck into the Wrift of his Right-hand, (which is the Gripe of a Mafter) and pulling it with all your Might, with your Right-foot to his Right-foot, and his Right-knee to your Right-knee, and his Right-breaft to your Right-breaft, and your Left-hand fupporting his Back, and whifper in his Ear, and fay, MAHHABONE; that is, almoft rotten to the Bone, which is the Mafter's Word.

Maf.

(59)

Maf. Brother, it feems that you could not be raifed but by the Five Points of Fellow-fhip : Pray will you explain them.

Anf. 1*ft.* Hand in Hand is, that I always will put forth my Hand to ferve a Brother as far as lies in my Power.

2*d.* Foot to Foot is, that I never will be a-fraid to go a Foot out of my Way to ferve a Brothe

3*d.* Knee to Knee is, that when I kneel down to Prayers, I ought never to forget to pray for my Brother as well as myfelf.

4*tb.* Breaft to Breaft, is to fhow I will keep my Brother's Secrets as my own.

5*tb.* The Left-hand fupporting the Back, is that I always will be willing to fupport a Bro-ther as far as lies in my Power.

The MASTER's Reasons.

Maf. WHY was you depriv'd of all Metal ?

Anf. Becaufe at the Building of *Solomon's* Temple, there was neither Axe, Hammer, or the Sound of any Metal Tool, heard in the Building of that wonderful Fabrick.

Maf. Why fo, Brother ?
Anf. Becaufe it fhould not be polluted.

Maf. How is it poffible, Brother, that fuch a large Building fhould be carry'd on, without the Sound of fome Metal Tool ?

I 2   *Anf.*

(60)

Anf. It was prepar'd in the Foreft of *Leba-non*, and brought down upon proper Carriages, and fet up with wooden Mauls made for that Purpofe.

Maf. Why was both your Shoes taken from off your Feet ?

Anf. Becaufe the Place whereon I ftood, when I was made a Mafon, was holy Ground ; for the Lord faid unto *Mofes*, pull off thy Shoes, for the Place whereon thou ftandeft is holy Ground.

Maf. What fupports your Lodge ?
Anf. Three great Pillars.

Maf. What are their Names ?
Anf. Wifdom, Strength and Beauty.

Maf. Who do they reprefent ?
Anf. Three Grand-Mafters ; *Solomon*, King of *Ifrael*, *Hiram*, King of *Tyre* ; and *Hiram Abiff*, which was the Widow's Son who was killed.

Maf. Were all thofe Three Grand Mafters concerned in the building of *Solomon*'s Temple ?
Anf. They were.

Maf. What was their Bufinefs ?
Anf. Solomon for finding Provifion, and Money to pay the Hirelings ; *Hiram*, King of *Tyre*, for finding Materials for the Work ; *Hiram Abiff*, for performing the Work.

[*Thus concludes the Mafter's Part, which is fufficient for all Lodges ; but fome will enlarge upon the aforefaid Parts, and run out of the Rules of Mafonry.*]

The

(61)

✳✳✳✳✳✳✳✳✳✳✳✳✳✳✳✳✳✳✳✳✳✳✳✳✳✳✳✳

The Charge given to the Officers of a Lodge.

AND firſt of the Maſter belonging to the Chair ; which they call inſtalling a Maſter for the Chair.

N. B. He kneels down in the South, upon both Knees ; and the late Maſter gives him the following Obligation, before he reſigns the Chair.

Anſ.   I *W----- V------.*

Of my own free Will and Accord, and in the Preſence of Almighty God, and this right worſhipful Lodge, dedicated to St. *John*, do hereby, and hereon, moſt ſolemnly and ſincerely ſwear, that I will not deliver the Word and Gripe belonging to the Chair whilſt I am in the Chair, or any Time hereafter, except it be to a Maſter in the Chair, or Paſt Maſter, him or them whom I ſhall find to be ſuch after juſt Trial and due Examination.

I furthermore do ſwear I will act as Maſter of this Lodge, till next St. *John*'s Day, and I will fill the Chair every Lodge Night, if I am within the Length of my Cable-Tow.

I alſo further promiſe that I will not wrong this Lodge, but I will do all Things for the Good of Maſonry in general ; nor will I reign arbitrarily, but I will be agreeable to the reſt of the Brethren. I alſo will keep good Orders in this Lodge, as far as lies in my Power, 'till next St. *Jhon*'s Day.

All

All this I fwear with a firm and fteady Re-folution to perform the fame, without any He-fitation in me whatfoever, under no lefs than the Four former Penalties, *viz.*

1*ft*. My Throat cut a-crofs, &c.

2*d*. My Tongue torn out, &c.

3*d*. Hy Heart torn from my Left-breaft, &c.

4*tb*. My Body fever'd in two, &c.

So help me God, and keep me ftedfaft in this my Obligation belonging to the Chair.

[*He kiffes the Book.*]

Then the late Mafter takes off his Jewel and puts it upon him, and takes him by the Mafter's Gripe, and raifes him off his Knees, and whifpers in his Ear the Word, which is CHIBBILUM, or, an excellent Mafon; then he flips his Hand from the Mafter's Gripe to his Elbow, and ftrikes his Nails in as you do in the other Gripe at the Wrift. This is the Word and Gripe belonging to the Chair.

N. B. The fenior and junior Warden, and Secretary, receive the fame Obligation as he in the Chair, only with this Difference, they have neither Gripe nor Word. Therefore I have no Occafion to infert it over again, as it is the fame, and the fame Penalties.

(63)

×××××××××××××××××××××××

The *MASTER*'s CLAP.

IS by holding both Hands above your Head,
and ſtriking upon your Apron, and both
Feet going at the ſame Time ready to ſhake
the Floor down: this they call the Grand Sign
of a Maſter Maſon. They give two Reaſons
for this Sign, *viz.* When they ſaw their Maſter *Hiram* lye dead, they lifted up their Hands
in a Surprize, and ſaid, O Lord, my God!
Second. When *Solomon* dedicated the Temple
to the Lord, he ſtood up, and lifting up both
his Hands, ſaid, O Lord my God, Great art
Thou above all Gods, for in this Hour will
I adore thy Name.

*Thus I finiſh the whole Three Degrees of the
moſt ancient* Free-Maſonry, *with the Gripe
and Word belonging to the Chair.*

How

(64)

XXXXXXXXXXXXXXXX·XXXXXXXXXX

How to go through an Examination, at the Door of a Free-Mason's *Lodge ; and get Admittance, though ever such a Stranger.*

WHEN you come to the Door of the Lodge, where the Tyler ſtands with a drawn Sword, aſk him if there is any Admittance ; he'll ſay, I will go in and aſk. Then the Maſter, or ſome other Man, will come out to prove you. Firſt draw your Right-hand edge-ways a-croſs your Throat ; he will ſay, what is that ? You ſay the due Guard of an enter'd Apprentice ; then he will take you by the firſt Joint of your Right-hand, and preſs upon it with his Right-thumb Nail, and ſay, what is this?

Anſ. The Gripe of an enter'd Apprentice.

Maſ. Has it got a Name ?
Anſ. It has.

Maſ. Will you give it me ?
Anſ. I'll Letter it with you, or half it.

Maſ. Begin.
Anſ. B O-
Maſ. A Z.
Anſ. B O A Z.

Maſ. Will you be off or from ?
Anſ. From.

Maſ.

(65)

Maf. From what ?

Anf, From an enter'd Apprentice to a Fel;
low-Craft.

N. B. Then he will put his Thumb from
off the Apprentice's Gripe towards the Crafts,
or between both.

Maf. What's this ?

Anf. The Pafs-Word of a Craft.

Maf. Will you give it me ?

Anf. SHIBBOLETH.

Maf. Pafs SHIBBOLETH.

N. B. Then he puts his Thumb to the fecond Joint, and fays what's this ?

Anf. The Gripe of a Fellow-Craft.

Maf. Has it got a Name ?

Anf. It has.

Maf. Will you give it me ?

Anf. I'll Letter it with you, or half it with
you.

Maf. I'll Letter it with you.

Anf. Begin.

Maf. No, you begin.

Anf. J

Maf. A

Anf. C

Maf. H

Anf. I

Maf. N.

Anf. JACHIN is the Word you demanded.

Maf. Will you be off or from ?

Anf. From.

Maf. From what ?

Anf. From a Craft to a Mafter,

K

Maf.

(66)

Maſ. Give me the Fellow-Craft's Sign?

N. B. Put your Right-hand to your Left-breaſt, your Thumb upright, and your Left-hand above your Head, forming a Square, then he takes you by the Maſter's Gripe.

Maſ. What's this?
Anſ. The Gripe of a Maſter Maſon.

Maſ. Has it got a Name?
Anſ. It has, and ſomething elſe thereunto belonging.

Maſ. What is that, Brother, as I may venture to call you ſo now, I believe.
Anſ. The Five Points of Fellowſhip.

Maſ. Will you give me them, Brother?

N. B. Firſt draw your Hand a-croſs your Belly, then lift both Hands up above your Head, and ſay, O Lord my God, and then take him by the Maſter's Gripe, which is your Right-hand to his Right-hand, and put your Right-foot to his Right-foot, your Right-knee to his Right-knee, your Right-breaſt to his Right-breaſt, and your Left-hand to his Back, and whiſper in his Ear, and ſay, MAHHABONE.

This is the Five Points of Fellowſhip, and Word and Gripe thereunto belonging, as has been before deſcrib'd. Theſe are all the Signs, Gripes and Words, that are uſed amongſt Maſons at this Day.

All

(67)

All the Words explained that belongs to the GRIPES.

In *Hebrew* thus

The APPREN-TICE's Word is BOAZ.	בֹּעַז	It fignifies Strength, and it belongs to the Senior-Warden. You may have feen him carry it at Burials.
The CRAFT's Word is JACHIN.	צָכִין	This fignifies to eftablifh in the Lord, and it belongs to the Junior Warden. They are about twenty Inches long, to reprefent the two Pillars, Boaz and Jachin, as aforefaid.
The CRAFT's Pafs-Word is SHIBBOLETH.	שִׁבֹּלֶת	This fignifies Plenty, or an Ear of Corn and Fall of Water, which is Peace and Plenty. The Battle was fought in a Corn-Field, near a Fall of Water. This Word difcovers the Enemy. Vide the Twelfth Chapter of Judges.
The MASTER's Word is MAHHABONE.	מֹחֻבֹּן	This fignifies rotten, or decayed almoft to the Bone. It is the Word that is whifpered in your Ear at the raifing of your Mafter, and is never to be fpoke out; for they receive it as folemn as the Name of God.
The MASTER's Pafs-Word is TUBALCAIN.	טֻבֹּלכֹּן	The Signification of this is, that he was the Inventor of Brafs, Iron, and other Metals: His Father was the Father of Mufick: He rofe from Cain, of the Fifth Generation; and his Son, Tubalcain, became excellent in all Metals, which Hiram improved. Vide the Fourth Chapter of Genefis.

NOTE.

(68)

N O T E.

THE Mafter always fits in the Eaft, or ftands with the Bible before him; and if it is the Apprentices Lecture, he opens it about the Second Epiftle of *Peter*, with the Compaffes laid thereon, and the Points of them covered with a little Box Square or *Lignum Vitæ*, about 4 Inches each Way, and the Points of the Compaffes points to the Weft, and the Two Points of the Square points to the Eaft. If it is the Craft's Lecture, the Mafter fhews one Point of the Compaffes, the Bible being open the 12th Chapter of *Judges*. If it is the Mafter's Lecture, the Bible is opened about the 7th Chap. of the Firft Book of *Kings*, and both the Points of the Compaffes is fhewn upon the Square. This is the Form they fit in when they work, as they call it.

The Reafon of their drinking Three Times Three is, becaufe there were antiently but Three Words, Three Signs and Three Gripes; but there have been Three added, *viz.* The Grand Sign of a Mafter, the Pafs-Gripe of a Fellow-Craft, and Pafs-Word, which is Twelve in all for you to remember, *viz.* The Word, Sign and Gripe of an enter'd Apprentice is Three : The Word, Sign, Gripe, Pafs-Gripe and Pafs-Word of a Fellow-Craft is Five: and the Mafter hath Four, *viz.* The Sign, the Grand Sign, the Gripe and Word, which is Twelve, as aforefaid.

F I N I S.

(69)

A New and Correct L<small>IST</small> of all the *Englifh* R<small>EGULAR</small> L<small>ODGES</small> in *Europe*, *Afia*, *Africa*, and *America*, according to their Seniority and Conftitution.

By Order of the G<small>RAND</small> M<small>ASTER</small>.

Brought down to the Year 1768.

N. B. In the following LIST, M ftands for Monday, Tu for Tuefday, W for Wednefday, Th for Thurfday, F for Friday, Sa for Saturday.

1 Q<small>UEEN</small>'s Arms, St. Paul's Church-Yard, 2d W. Every 4th W there is a Mafter's Lodge. It is alfo the Weft-India and American Lodge.

2 Horn, Weftminfter, 2d Th. Both the above conftituted Time immemorial.

3 Thatched Houfe, St. James's Street, Lodge of Friendfhip, Jan. 17, 1721.

4 Crown and Rolls, Chancery-lane, 2d and 4th Tu. Jan. 19, 1721.

5 Angel, St. Mary le Bonne, 1ft Th, Jan. 28, 1721.

6 Salmon and Ball, Charles-ftreet, Soho-fquare, 1ft and 3d W, Feb. 27, 1722.

8 Running Horfe, David-Street, Grofvenor-fquare, 4th W, May, 1722-3.

9 Dundee-Arms, at their own Private-Room, Wapping, 2d and 4th Th, 1722.

10 Mitre, in Globe lane, Chatham, 1ft and 3d M, March 28, 1723.

11 King's Arms, Wandfworth, 1ft Tu, March 30, 1723.

12 Three Crowns, Eaft Smithfield, 2d and 4th F, April 1, 1723.

13 Feathers, Cheapfide, late the Mourning Bufh, 2d and 4th Monday, 1723.

14 Crown and Rolls, Chancery-Lane, 2d and 4th Th, Aug. 4, 1723,

15 Golden Anchor, at the Ballaft Key, in Eaft Greenwich, 2d and 4th Tu, Sept. 11, 1723.

16 Globe, Fleet-Street, 1ft Th, Sept. 18, 1723.

17 Swan, Whitecrofs ftreet, Hatton-Garden, 4th Th, Oct. 20, 1723,

L   18Pewter

18 Pewter Platter, Crofs-ftreet, Hatton Garden, 2d and 4th Th, Dec. 24, 1723.

19 Thatched Houfe, Norwich, St. Lawrences Parifh, 1ft Th, 1724.

20 Dolphin, Chichefter, 3d W. July 17, 1724.

21 Three Tuns, Portfmouth, 1ft and 3d F, four o'Clock, 1724,

22 George, Ironmonger Lane, 2d and 4th M, Jan. 22, 1724.

23 Queen's Head, at Stockton upon Tees, County of Durham, 1ft and 3d F, Feb. 1724.

24 Sun, Ludgate-ftreet, 1ft and 3d M, April 1725.

25 Crofs Keys, Henrietta-Street, Covent-Garden, 1ft and 3d Tu, May 23, 1725.

26 St. Alban, St. Alban-Street, 3d M, Jan. 31, 1727.

27 Three Fleur de-Luce's, St. Barnard Street, Madrid, 1ft Su, 1727.

28 Crown, little Cranbourn-Alley, Leicefter Fields, 1ft and 3d Th, 1728.

29 Swan, Elephant Stairs, Rotherhith, 2d Th, 1728.

30 Gibralter, at Gibralter, 1ft Tu, Nov. 1728.

31 Lion, Lynn Regis, Norfolk, 1ft F, Oct. 1, 1729.

32 ———— Jan. 22, 1729.

33 ———— Jan. 24, 1729.

34 Albermarle Arms, Dover Street, 2d and 4th Tu, March 25, 1730.

35 ————

36 Red Crofs, Barbican, 1ft W, 3d a Mafter's Lodge, May 22, 1730.

37 White Lion, Putney, Th, neareft full Moon, July 17, 1730.

38 ———— Sept. 7, 1730.

39 King of Pruffia, Anchor Street, Bethnal-green, 1ft Friday, Jan. 26, 1730.

40 ————

41 Old Magpye, Bifhopfgate-Street, 2d M, 1730.

42 Wind Mill, Rofemary Lane, 1ft M, 1730.

43 Angel, Macclesfield, Chefhire, 1731.

44 St. John of Jerufalem, Clerkenwell, 3d and 4th W, Dec. 17, 1731.

45 ————

46 Salutation and Cat, Newgate-Street, 1ft and 3d M, Jan. 11, 1731.

47 King's Arms, St. Margaret's Hill, Southwark, 3d M, Feb. 2, 1731.

48 Green

A LIST of Regular Lodges.   7**1**

48 King's Arms, Leigh in Lancashire, Feb. 22.

49 A la Ville de Tonerre, Rue des Boucheries a Paris, 1st M, April 3, 1732.

50 Turk's Head, Gerrard Street, Soho, 2d and 4th Tu, May 25, 1732.

51 King's Arms, Mary-le-bone Street, Picadilly, 2d and 4th Tu, Jan. 12, 1732.

52 Bacchus and Tun, at Hoxton, 3d, Th, June 12, 1732.

53 Lion and Cock, St. Michael's Alley, Cornhill, 3d Tu, Sept. 8, 1732.

54 Royal Oak, Darby, 1st and 3d Tu, Sept. 14, 1732.

55 Anchor and Hope Lodge, Bolton-le-more, Lancashire, Th. on or before Full Moon, Nov. 9. 1732.

56 Three Swans, Salisbury, 1st and 3d W, Dec. 27, 1732.

57 West-Cowes, Isle of Wight, 2d and 4th M, Feb. 17, 1732.

58 Swan, Chelsea, 2d and 4th Th, March 3, 1732.

59 White Bear, Bath, 1st and 3d Tu, May 18, 1733.

60 Mitre, Fleet-Street, 1st and 3d M, May 23, 1733.

61 Red Lion, Bury, Lancashire, next Th. to every Full Moon, July 26, 1733.

62 Talbot, Stourbich, Worcestershire, every W, Aug. 1, 1733.

63 Sun, St. Paul's Church Yard, 2d and 4th W, December 27, 1733.

64 King's Head, New Street, Birmingham, 1st and 3d F, 1733.

65 Royal Exchange, Boston, New-England, 2d and 4th Sa, 1733.

66 Valenciennes, French Flanders, 1733.

67 Oxford Inn, Plimouth Dock, 1st and 3d W, 1734.

68 Strong Man, East-Smithfield, late the Ship at the Hermitage, 1st and 3d Th, Feb. 17, 1734.

69 King's Head near the Watch-House, High Holbourn, 2d and 4th W, June 11, 1735.

70 Horn, Fleetstreet, Steward's Lodge, Publick Nights, 3d W in March and September.

71 In Holland, 1735.

72 Dorothy Jones's, in Swalewell, near Newcastle upon Tyne, 1st M, June 24, 1735.

73 Castle, at Aubigney in France, 1st M, Aug. 12, 1735.

74 Nov.

74 Nov. 12, 1735.

75 Savannah, at Savannah, in the Province of Georgia, 1735.

76 Angel, Colc. efter, 2d and 4th M, 1735.

77 Fountain, Gatefhead, Newcaftle upon Tyne, 2d and 4th W, March 8, 1735.

78 Green Man, Shrewsbury, 1ft M, April 16, 1736.

79 Rifing Sun, Fafhion Street, Spittle Fields, 2d and 4th W, June 11, 1736.

80 King's Head, Norwich, laft Thurfday, 1736.

81 Th. Cuftom Houfe by the Dock, Liverpool, 1ft W, June 25, 1736.

82 Orange Tree, Bloomsbury-Square, 1ft M, Aug. 16, 1736.

83 Swan, Wolverhampton, 1ft and 3d Tu, Sept. 20, 1736.

84 Half Moon, Cheapfide, 2d and 4th F, Dec. 2, 1736.

85 Star, ColemanStreet, 1ft and 3d M, Dec. 21, 1736.

86 Caveac Tavern, Spread Eagle Court, Finch lane, Cornhill, 2d and 4th W, Dec. 31, 1736.

87 ————Jan. 24, 1736.

88 ————Feb 14. 1736.

89 Three Tuns, Spittlefields, 2d and 4th F, April 18, 1737.

90 Chapman's Coffee Houfe, Sackville Street, 1ft and 3d Tu, Aug. 24, 1737.

91 Talbot Inn, Strand, 1ft Tu, Sept. 21, 1737.

92 Sun, Milk Street, Honey Lane-Market, 1ft and 3d Tu, Dec. 8, 1737.

93 Angel, Shipton Mallet, Somerfetfhire, 1ft and 3d M, Dec. 12, 1737.

94 Parham Lodge, Parham, Antigua, Jan. 31, 1737.

95 Swan, Gloucefter, 1ft and 3d F, March 28, 1738.

96 Crown Tavern, Leadenhall Street, 2d Tu, May 3, 1738.

97 Rofe and Crown, Halifax, in Yorkfhire, 2d and 4th W, July 12, 1738.

98 The great Lodge at St. John's, Antigua, 2d and 4th W, Nov. 22, 1738.

99 Fox, near the Square, Manchefter, 2d and 4th M, 1738.

100 Three Compaffes, High-Holbourn, 2d and 4th M, Jan. 27, 1738.

101 Coach and Horfes, Watergate Street, Chefter, 2d Tu, Feb. 1, 1738.

103 Red

A LIST of Regular Lodges.   73

103 Red Lion, Hornchurch, in Essex, 1ft P, March 13, 1738.

104 Baker's Lodge, St. Mary's Street, St. John's Antigua, March 14, 1738.

105 The Mother Lodge, Kingston, Jamaica, 1ft and 3d Sa, April 14, 1739.

106 April 24, 1739.

107 Scotch Arms, the Mother Lodge, at St. Chriftopher's, held at Baffeterre, 1ft Th, June 21, 1739.

108 Crown and Ball, Playhoufe-Yard, Black Friars, 1ft Tu, Aug. 24, 1739,

109 Eaft India Arms, John Street, Blacks-Fields, Horfleydown, 1ft and 3d W, Oct. 8, 1739.

110 Albemarle Arms, South-Audley Street, 2d and 4th W, Oct. 25, 1739.

111 Queen's Head, Grays-Inn Gate, Holbourn, 3d M, Dec. 7, 1739.

112 King's Head, in the Poultry, 3d W, Jan. 1739.

113 Private Room, Laufanne, in the Canton of Bern in Switzerland, Feb. 2, 1739.

114 Three Lyons, Banbury, Oxfordfhire, every Full-Moon, if on Th, or the Th, before, March 31, 1740.

115 Ship, James Street, Covent-Garden, 2d Tu, June 26, 1740.

116 Fountain, High Street, Briftol, 1ft and 3d To, July 10, 1740.

117 The Third Lodge, at Calcutta, in the Eaft-Indies 1740.

118 St. Michael's Lodge, in Barbadoes, 1740.

119 Bunch of Grapes, Decker-ftreet, Hamburgh, every other Th, Oct. 23, 1740.

120 George, Whitehaven, Cumberland, 2d M, March 19, 1740.

121 Three Cranes, High-ftreet, Haverford Weft, South Wales, April 24, 1741.

122 Two Chairmen, Little Warwick Street, Chairing Crofs, 2d and 4th Th, in Winter, 2d Th, in Summer, April 13, 1742.

123 Old Road, at St. Chriftophers, Jan. 17, 1742.

124 Union, Franckfort in Germany, 2d and 4th Tu, Jan. 17, 1742.

125 Three Horfe Shoes, Leominfter, in the County of Hereford, Oct. 11, 1742.

126 Port Royal Lodge, Jamaica, 1742.

127

127 Angel, Dolgelly in Merionethſhire, North-Wales, 1ſt Tu, Sept. 17, 1743.

128 St. George, Emperor's Court, Hamburgh, every other W,˙ Septı 24, 1743.

129 ⸺⸺⸺⸺

130 New Lodge at Copenhagen, Denmark, Oct 25. 1745.

131 St. Jago de la Vego, in Jamaica, April 29,1746.

132 Angel, Norwich, 2d and 4th Tu, May 9, 1747.

133 A new Lodge in St. Euſtatia, Dutch Iſland, Weſt-Indies, June 6, 1747.

134 Prince George's Head, Plimouth, 1ſt and 3d M, May 1, 1748.

135 ⸺⸺⸺ June 15, 1748.

136 Queen's Head, Norwich, 3d Tu, Jan. 5, 1749.

137 Sun, at Cambridge, 2d M, March, 31, 1749.

138 Lodge of Orange, at Rotterdam, May 5, 1764.

139 St. Martin's Lodge, at Copenhagen, in Denmark, Oct. 9, 1749.

140 Sun, St. Peter's Mancroft, Norwich, 2d and 4th W, Jan. 9, 1749.

141 ⸺⸺⸺

142 ⸺⸺⸺

143 ⸺⸺⸺

144 St. Chriſtopher's, at Sandy Point, July 20, 1750.

145 King and Miller, St. Bennet's Norwich, 2d and 4th W, Feb. 12, 1751.

146 King's Arms, Falmouth, 2d and 4th Th, May 20, 1751.

147 Angel, Great Yarmouth, in Norfolk, June 6, 1751.

148 King's Head, Weſt-Street, Gravefend, 1ſt and 3d Th, June 8, 1751.

149 King's Head, Fenchurch-ſtreet, the Sea Captain's Lodge, 3d Tu, Aug. 29, 1751.

150 ⸺⸺⸺

151 King's Arms, at Helſton in Cornwall, in Cornwall, 1ſt and 3d Tu, April 14, 1752.

152 St. John's Lodge, at Bridge Town, in the Iſland of Barbadoes, 4th M, April 23, 1752.

153 Ship, Leadenhall-ſtreet, late the Bell at Aldgate, 2d and 4th M, July 13, 1752.

154 The George, the Corner of Maggot's Court, Piccadilly, 3d Tu, Aug. 21, 1753.

155

A LIST of REGULAR LODGES.   75

155 Mafon's Arms, at Truro, in Cornwall, 1ft and 3d Tu, Sept. 22, 1752.

157 At Chardenagore, the Chief French Settlement, in Bengal, Eaft-India.

157 At Madrafs, in Eaft-India.

158 At the Hague, in Holland.

159 St. Peter's Lodge, in the Ifland of Barbadoes, 1ft and 3d Sa. Dec. 15, 1752.

160 Jan. 7, 1753.

161 Lion and Goat, Grofvenor Street, 2d and 4th M, Feb. 24, 1753.

162 Crown and Horfefhoe, Corner of Bartlet's Buildings, Holbourn, 2d W, March 5, 1751.

163 White Hart, Shug Lane, Piccadilly, 1ft M.

164 Lilly Tavern, Guernfey, May 10, 1753.

165 Nag's Head, Wine Street, Briftol, 2d and 4th Tu, Auguft 22, 1753.

166 Vine, High Holbourn, 2d and 4th Tu, in Winter, and 4th Th, in Summer, Oct. 23, 1753.

167 Shakefpear, Market Street, Carmarthen, South Wales, 1ft and 3d M, Oct. 24, 1753.

168 King's Head, Prince's Street, Cavendifh Square, 2d and 4th W, Nov. 5. 1753.

169 Church Style, St. Peter's Mancroft, Norwich, 3d W, Nov. 10, 1753.

170 Evangelift's Lodge, at Antigua, Nov. 10, 1753.

171 At Amfterdam, Nov. 30, 1753.

172 Royal Oak at Prefcot, in Lancafhire, W next before Full Moon, Dec. 20, 1753.

173 The Royal Exchange Lodge, in the Borough of Norfolk, Virginia, 1ft Th, Dec. 22, 1753.

174 Jan. 31, 1754.

175 Crown, Holywell Lane, Shoreditch, 1ft M.

176 Private Room, at Redrath, in Cornwall, 1ft and 3d Th, Feb. 14, 1754.

177 Feb. 18, 1754.

178 Mitre, Union Street, Weftminfter, 2d Tu, March 2, 1754.

179 Three Tuns, North Cornsford, Norwich, 1ft and 3d Monday, March 4, 1754.

180 Swan, Ramfgate, in the Ifle of Thanet, 2d and 4th M, March 8, 1754.

181

181 Parrot, Cow-Lane, in Leeds, firſt Wedneſday, March 28, 1754.

182 Three Tuns, Cambridge, 4th M, March 28, 1754.

183 The Angel and Porter, Golden Lane, Barbican, firſt Monday, April 5, 1754.

184 Marquis of Granby's Head, near St. George's Church, Southwark, 1ſt Wedneſday, April 13, 1754.

185 ―――― May 13, 1754.

186 Three Compaſſes and Punch Bowl, Silver-ſtreet, Golden Square, 2d and 4th Thurſday, June 4, 1754.

187 Pelican, Leiceſter, firſt and third Tueſday, Aug. 21, 1754.

188 Bear, Cardiffe, Glamorganſhire, South Wales, ſecond M, Auguſt 1754.

188 Bear, Cowbridge, Glamorganſhire, laſt Monday, Sept. 1754.

190 No. 2. St. Euſtatia, Dutch Iſland, Weſt Indies, 1754

191 Queen's Head, Lowſtoffe, in Suffolk, ſecond Monday, October 29, 1754.

192 Chequers, Chairing Croſs, ſecond Tueſday, November 2, 1754.

193 Horn, Doctor's Commons, 2d and 4th Monday, December 14, 1754.

194 Crompton's Coffee houſe, Mancheſter, firſt and third Thurſday, Feb. 4, 1755.

195 No. 8. the King's own Regiment of Foot, firſt and third Tueſday, February 15, 1755.

196 Turk's Head, King-ſtreet, Bloomsbury, ſecond and fourth Friday in Winter, ſecond Friday in Summer, March 2, 1755.

197 Jack of Newbury, Chiſwell Street, firſt and 3d Wedneſday, April 5, 1755.

198 Horſeſhoe, in Jermyn ſtreet, 2d and 4th Friday, May 5, 1755.

199 Star, Penzance, in Cornwall, 2d and 4th Wedneſday, June, 14, 1755.

200 King's Arms, Tower Street, Seven Dials, firſt and third Monday, June 17, 1755.

201 The Duke, St. Bennet, Norwich, firſt and third Monday, June 17, 1755.

202 The Lodge of Charity at Amſterdam, June 24, 1755.

203

A LIST of Regular Lodges.

203 Eagle and Castle, Chester, every other Monday, June 24, 1755.

204 Lion, Beccles, in Suffolk, July 14, 1755.

205 Swan Tavern in York Town, Virginia, 1st and third Wednesday, August 1, 1755.

206 The Twins, Norwich, first and third Friday, Sept. 16, 1755.

207 Nag's Head, Sunderland, Durham, first Friday, Oct. 7, 1755.

208 The Grand Lodge Fredrick, at Hanover, Nov. 25, 1755.

209 Dog and Bull, Northgate-street, Chester, December 2, 1755.

210 Swan, Rider's Court, Cranborne-Alley, Leicester Fields, first and third Monday, Jan. 20, 1756.

211 A Lodge in Capt. Bell's Troop, in the Right Hon. Lord Ancram's Regiment of Dragoons, February 7, 1755.

212 Crown and Anchor, Strand, 2d and 4th Friday, Feb. 26, 1751.

213 A Lodge at Wilmington, on Cape Fear River, in the Province of North Carolina, March, 1755.

214 Merlin's Cave, Old Shambles, Liverpool, April, 15, 1755.

215 The Lodge of Peace at Amsterdam, September, 23, 1756.

216 ———— April 30, 1756.

217 White Horse, Corner of New Burlington Street, first and third Thursday, December 2, 1756.

218 At the Marquis of Carnavon, at Sunderland, first and third Tuesday, January 14, 1757.

219 In the Parish of St. Mary, in the Island of Jamaica, Feb. 17, 1757.

220 Nag's Head, Vine Street, Bristol, second and fourth Thursday, February 17, 1757.

221 At Parliament Coffee-House, Parliament Street, second and fourth Wednesday, Feb. 14, 1757.

222 Star, at Lynn Regis, in Norfolk, 4th Wednesday, Feb. 21, 1757.

223 Dove and Branch, in the Parish of St. Lawrence, Norwich, second Wednesday, March 23, 1757.

224 Sancta Croix, Danish Island in the West-Indies, 1756.

225 Cock, the Head of the Side, Newcastle upon Tyne, first Monday, October 13, 1737.

M   226

A LIST of Regular Lodges.

226 Bacchus's Tun, Bloomsbury Market, second Monday, May 14, 1757.

227 Sun, at Shadwell, first and third Monday, Oct. 31, 1757.

228 The Lodge of Regularity, at Amsterdam, Nov. 21, 1757.

229 Long-Acre Coffee-house, first and third Friday, Dec. 20, 1757.

230 St. Michael's Lodge, in the City of Schwerin, in the Dutchy of Mecklenburg, May 15, 1754.

231 Cock, in the Parish of St. Mary, Norwich, every other Saturday, February 18, 1758.

232 Three Crowns, Southside Street, Plymouth, second and fourth Monday, March 1, 1758.

233 Duke of Beaufort, on the Quay, Bristol, second and fouth Tuesday, March 8, 1758.

234 Lodge at Bombay, in the East Indies, March 24, 1758.

235 Mercer's Arms, Mercer's Street, Long Acre, third Wednesday, August 6, 1758.

236 Swan at Yarmouth, Norfolk, the Sea Captain's Lodge, January 1, 1759.

237 Three Crowns at Plymouth, the second Division of Marines, January 2, 1759.

238 St. James's Lodge, at Barbadoes, May 20, 1758.

239 New Inn, at Exeter, second and last Friday, 1752.

240 Sun, at Newton Abbot, Devonshire, second Tuesday, March 17, 1759.

241 The Angel, in the West Town of Crediton, Devon, first Monday, April 21, 1759.

242 Royal Oak, Portsmouth Common, second and fourth Friday, April 21, 1759.

243 Compass and Square, Barnard Castle, Durham, first Monday, April 21, 1759.

244 Mermaid, at Windsor, third Monday, June 6, 1759.

245 Temple Lodge, at Bristol, first and third Monday, July 2, 1759.

246 Lebeck's Head in the Strand, third Friday Aug. 24, 1759.

247 Prince George Lodge, in George Town Winyau, South Carolina, once a Month, 1743.

248 Union Lodge, Charles Town, South Carolina, second and fourth Thursday, May 3, 1755.

249

A LIST of REGULAR LODGES.

249 A Mafter's Lodge, Charles Town, South Ca-rolina, fecond and fourth Thurfday, March 22, 1756.

250 Port Royal, at Beaufort, Port Royal Carolina, every other Wednefday, September 15, 1756.

251 ———————

252 Black Bull, at Mighton's Gate, Hull, fecond and laft Thurfday, Auguft 20, 1759.

253 King's Head, Canterbury, 1ft and 3d Wednef-day, Jan. 14, 1763.

254 A Lodge on board the Vanguard, January 16, 1760.

255 St. Andrew's Crofs, the Marines Lodge, near the Hermitage, firft and third Friday.

256 Three Crowns, at Guernfey, firft and third Mon day.

257 Guy Earl of Warwick, Gray's-Inn-Lane, firft Friday, Nov. 27, 1760.

258 Golden Lyon, near the Bridge, Leeds, York fhire, fecond Wednefday and Fourth, a Mafter's Lodge, January 8. 1761.

259 Punch Bowl, Stone Gate, York, 1ft and 3d Monday, Jan. 12, 1761.

260 Feathers, Cheapfide, the Caledonian Lodge, firft and third Thurfday, March 9, 1761.

261 Square and Compafs, Whitehaven, Cumberland, fecond Monday, May 4, 1761.

262 Lord Granby's Head, Dover, 1ft and 3d Thurf-day, May 8, 1761.

263 Sun, at Darlington, Yorkfhire, laft Saturday, June 19, 1761.

264 Spread Eagle, Wifbich, firft and third Tuefday, Aug. 8, 1761.

265 ———————, Aug. 20, 1761.

266 Union Lodge, Crow Lane, Barbadoes, firft Wednefday, September 17, 1761.

267 A Lodge at Kingfton upon Hull, fecond and fourth Thurfday, Oct. 27, 1761.

268 All Saints Lodge, at Wooler, Northumberland, January 1, 1762.

269 St. George's Lodge, at the Half Moon, Exeter, fecond and fourth Friday, January 20, 1762.

270 Green Man, Ipfwich, Suffolk, January 21, 1762.

271 Royal Fredrick, at Rotterdam, Jan. 25, 1726.

272 No. 2, St. John's Lodge, New York, fecond and fourth Wednefday, December 27, 1757.

M 2   273

A LIST of REGULAR LODGES.

273. George, Birmingham, 1ft. and 3d. Tu, Feb. 23, 1762.

274. A Private Room, at Appledore, Devon, March 18, 1762.

275. Eighth lodge at Calcutta, in the Eaft Indies, Feb. 7, 1761.

276. Hole in the Wall, at Colne, Lancafhire.

277. The Merchants Lodge, at Quebec, Mar. 2, 1762.

278. ——, May 8, 1762.

279. Somerfet-houfe Lodge, at the King's Arms, New Bond-ftreet, May 22, 1762.

280. Globe, High-ftreet, Salop, 1ft. and 3d. Wednefday, May 28, 1762.

281 Fleece, at Barnftable, Devon. 1ft. and 3d. Monday, May 28, 1762.

282 Eaft India Arms, at Deal, June 8, 1762.

283 Duke's Head, Lynn Regis, Norfolk, third Friday, June 9, 1762.

284 La Loge des Freres Réunis, at Amfterdani, June 16, 1762.

285 Lodge of Inhabitants of Gibraltar, July 12,1762.

286 St. David's Lodge, King's Head and Mafon's Arms, Holywell, North Wales, fecond and fourth Wednefday, January 13, 1761.

287 Half moon, at Otley, in Yorkfhire, firft Monday, Auguft 16, 1762.

288 Virtutis & Artis Amici, at Amfterdam, September 16. 1762.

289 At Workington, in Cumberland, firft Monday, September 22, 1762.

290 Green Dragon, at Hereford, firft Thurfday, October 12, 1756.

291 King's Arms, Portfmouth, 1ft and 3d Monday, November 2, 1762.

292 Feathers, Market Place, Nottingham, 3d Tuefday, Jan. 31, 1763.

293 The Sun, Univerfity Lodge, Cambridge, fecond Thurfday March 1, 1763.

294 Crown, Rochefter, 2d and 4th Friday, Mar. 17, 1763

295 Black Bull, at Hexam, Northumberland, firft and third Wednefday, March 8, 1763.

296 Stag, at Chippenham, Perfect Union Lodge, 1ft Monday, Mafter's Lodge, third Tuefday, May 1763.

297 Lodge at Richmond, Yorkfhire, fecond Monday, May 4, 1763.

298

A LIST of REGULAR LODGES.

298 Bear, at Havant, in Hampshire, 1st and 3d Wednesday, 1763.

299 St. Mark's Lodge, South Carolina, Feb. 8, 1763.

300 The Lodge of Regularity, at St. John's Hall, Black River, Musquito Shore, first and third Tuesday, March 8, 1763

301 City of London, at Dover, first and third Wednesday, August 2, 1763.

302 Lodge in a private Room, at Stubbington, Hants, Aug. 10, 1763.

303 Seven Stars, in the parish of St. Thomas the Apostle, near Exeter, 1st and 3d Wed. Aug. 10, 1763.

304 Marquiss of Granby's Head, Durham, first Tuesday, September 8. 1763.

305 Lodge at the Hall at Burnley, Lancashire, every Saturday nearest the Full Moon, October 9, 1763.

306 The Union Lodge, at the Coopers Arms, in Camomile-street, Bishopsgate-street, first and third Saturday, November 7, 1763.

307 Royal Mecklenburgh Lodge, at the Hermione, and Active Frigate, Compton-street, St. Ann's, fourth Friday, November 28, 1763.

308 Sarracen's Head, Chelmsford, Essex, second and fourth Monday, January 18, 1764.

309 Lodge of Amity, at the Haul Over, up the River Belise, in the Bay of Honduras, first and third Tuesday, September 21, 1763.

310 Faulcon, East-street, Gravesend, second and fourth Thursday, March 4, 1764.

311 Royal Edwin Lodge, at Lyme Regis, in Dorsetshire, first and third Monday, April 6, 1764.

312 The Door to Virtue, at Hildesheim in Germany, Dec. 27, 1762.

313 Royal Lodge, Thatched House, St. James's-street, late the New Lodge, at the Horn, Westminster, first Wednesday, April 4, 1764.

314 Vitruvian Lodge, Swan and Faulcon, Rofs, Herefordshire, May 3, 1764.

315 St. George's Lodge, at Taunton, Somersetshire, July 13, 1764.

316 Swan, at Kendal, Westmorland, first Wednesday, July 31, 1764.

317 Three Crowns, at Harwich, second and fourth Thursday, August 9, 1764.

318 Nag's Head, at Lymington, Hants, first and third Friday, August 16, 1764.

319

A LIST of Regular Lodges.

319 White Hart, at Melton, in Kent, every other Wednesday, August 28, 1764.

320 Salutation, at Topsham, Devon, second and fourth Wednesday, August 30, 1764.

321 Globe, St. Saviour's Church-yard, Southwark, second Tuesday, October 23, 1764.

322 Club Inn, Isle of Ely, first Wednesday, October 23, 1764.

323 Fountain, at Helsey, Hants, first and third Monday, Nov. 7, 1764.

324 Pon's Coffee-house, Castle-street, Leicester-fields, second and fourth Monday.

325 Half Moon, Cheapside, Caledonian Lodge, first Monday, November 15, 1764.

326 Swan, at Bridgwater, Somerset, first and third Monday, December 4, 1764.

327 Rose and Crown, Mill-street, Dock Head, Southwark, first and third Tuesday, December 11, 1764.

328 Rose, at Sittingbourn, in Kent, first and third Tuesday.

329 Crown, at Swaffham, Norfolk, first Monday, December 17, 1764.

330 King of Sweden, Wapping Dock, first and third Tuesday, January 8, 1765.

331 Fountain, Ludgate Hill, French Lodge, second and fourth Thursday, January 20, 1765.

332 Boar's Head Lodge, at the Fountain, Snow-hill, first and third Wednesday, January 29, 1765.

333 Goose and Gridiron, St. Paul's Church-yard, first and third Thursday, January 29, 1765.

334 Dolphin and Horseshoe, Lamb's-conduit-passage, Red-lion-street, third Friday, January 22, 1765.

335 George, Wardour-street, Soho, Operative Masons, first and third Tuesday, March 13, 1765.

336 George, Shug-lane, fourth Monday, March 22, 1765.

337 Bell, Brecon, South Wales, first and third Monday.

338 Lion and Lamb, Pool, Dorset, 1st and 3d Wednesday, April 1, 1765.

339 White Hart, Strand, April 16, 1765.

340 Rose and Crown, Sheffield, Yorkshire, second Friday, April 19, 1765.

341 At Alost, in Flanders, June 5, 1765.

342 Rose and Crown, Coventry, first and third Monday, June 20, 1765.

343

87

A LIST of Regular Lodges.

343 Queen's Head, Chelfea, fecond Friday in Summer, fecond and fourth in Winter, June 29, 1765.

344 White Lion, Rye, in Suffex, firft and third Tuefday, July 10, 1765.

345 Flafk, at Chelfea, third Tuefday, July 17, 1765.

346 Lodge at Joppa, in Baltimore County, Maryland, Auguft 8, 1765.

347 La Sageffe St. Andrew, at the Grenades, May 1, 1764.

348 Greyhound and Shakefpear Inn, and Tavern, at Bath.

349 A Lodge, No. 1. conftituted in the Town of St. Hilary, in the Ifland of Jerfey.

350 New Inn, Melkfham, Wilts, firft and third Wednefday, December 7, 1765.

351 At Tortola and Beef Ifland, firft and third Wednefday, December 7, 1765.

352 Fleece, at Warrington, in Lancafhire, laft Monday, November 8, 1765.

353 Lodge, No. 1. at Madrafs.

354 Lodge, No. 2. at Madrafs.

355 Lodge, No. 3. at Madrafs.

356 Lodge, No. 1. at Bencoolen.

357 Blue Boar, at Norwich.

358 Red Lion, (the Royal Edwin,) at Fakenham, in Norfolk, fecond Monday, and laft Monday a Mafter's Lodge, December 30, 1765.

359 Lodge of Perfeverance, at Amfterdam, 2d and 4th Saturday.

360 Ship, at St. Ive's, Cornwall, firft and third Tuefday, July 16, 1765.

361 George and Crown, at Wakefield, Yorkfhire, Feb. 15, 1766.

362 King's Arms Punch-houfe, Shad Thames, firft Monday, February 22, 1766.

363 Englifh Lodge, at Bourdeaux, met fince the Year 1732, March 8, 1766.

364 Mitre, (Operative Mafons,) Union-ftreet, Weftminfter, 2d and 4th Wednefday, May 17, 1766.

365 Dolphin, at Shoreham, firft and third Thurfday, April 18, 1766.

366 Black Lion, at Greenwich, 2d and 4th Tuefday, May 26. 1766.

367 White Hart Inn, Lewes, in Suffex, firft and third Wednefday, May 29, 1766.

368 Swan, Oxford-road, 3d Wed. June 23, 1766.

369

A LIST of Regular Lodges.

369 Recruiting Serjeant, Carlisle, Cumberland, first and third Friday, August 1, 1766.

370 Globe, at Exeter, August 6, 1766.

371 Weavers Arms, Dorset-street, Spitalfields, fourth Tuesday, July 26, 1766.

372 Union Lodge, Princes-street, opposite Merchants Hall, Bristol, 2d and 4th Wednesday, Sep. 9. 1766.

373 King's Head Tavern and Coffee-house, Islington, second Friday, September 10, 1766.

374 Black Horse, Oxendon-street, Haymarket, September 16, 1766.

375 Le Loge de Sagesse, a Havre, Normandie, en France, October 8, 1766.

376 Crown and Anchor Lodge, (constituted the Lodge of Immortality,) in the Strand, 1st and 3d Tu. 1766.

377 White Hart, Exeter, October 31, 1766.

378 St. Nicholas Lodge, (private Room,) Newcastle upon Tyne, November 29, 1766.

379 Sion Lodge, (private Room,) North Shields, Northumberland, November 29, 1766.

380 Thistle and Crown, near Tower-hill, second and fourth Monday, December 4, 1766.

381 Star, Water-gate-street, Chester, third Thursday, November 28, 1766.

382 Rose and Crown, (Lodge of Peace,) opposite the Custom-house, Thames-street, second and fourth Thursday, December 19, 1766.

383 King's Arms, Bennet-street, Southwark, (the Black Friars Bridge, Lodge,) second and fourth Tuesday, February 9 1767.

384 Castle, Holborn, February 16, 1767.

385 Upper Swan, Market-street-lane, Manchester, 1767

386 Sun, at Chatham, February 17, 1767.

387 White Hart, Folkstone in Kent, first and third Thursday, March 16, 1767.

388 Lodge at Grenoble, in France, March 18, 1767.

389 Admiral Hawke, Jerusalem Lodge, on the Quay, at Bristol, April 1, 1767.

390 The Constitution, Bedford-street, Covent garden, first and third Friday, April 11, 1767.

391 Bull's Head, Little Windmill-street.

F I N I S.

Jachin and Boaz

JACHIN AND BOAZ;

OR, AN

AUTHENTIC KEY

TO THE DOOR OF

FREE-MASONRY,

Both ANCIENT and MODERN.

Calculated not only for the Inſtruction of every New made MASON, but alſo for the Information of all who intend to become Brethren.

CONTAINING,

I. A circumſtantial Account of all the Proceedings in making a Maſon, with the ſeveral Obligations of an ENTERED APPRENTICE, FELLOW-CRAFT, and MASTER; the Prayers, and alſo the Sign, Grip, and Paſs-Word of each Degree, with the Ceremony of the Mop and Pail.

II. The Manner of opening a Lodge, and ſetting the Craft to work.

III. The *Entered Apprentice, Fellow-Craft*, and *Maſter's Lectures*, verbatim, as delivered in all Lodges; with the Song at the Concluſion of each Part.

IV. The Origin of Maſonry; Deſcription of *Solomon's* Temple; Hiſtory of the Murder of the Grand Maſter *Hiram* by the three Fellow-Crafts; their Diſcovery and Puniſhment; the Burial of *Hiram* by King *Solomon's* Order, with the Five Points of Fellowſhip, &c.

V. The Ceremony of the Inſtalment of the Maſters of different Lodges on St. *John's* Day,—Deſcription of the Regalia, &c.

VI. Ceremonies uſed at the Funeral of a Maſon.

VII. A ſafe and eaſy Method propoſed by which a Man may obtain Admittance into any Lodge, without paſſing through the Form required, and thereby ſave a Guinea or two in his Pocket.

VIII. Anthems, Odes, Songs, &c.

Illuſtrated with

A Beautiful FRONTISPIECE of the REGALIA, JEWELS, and Emblematical ORNAMENTS belonging to MASONRY.

AND

An Accurate Plan of the Drawing on the Floor of a Lodge,

Interſperſed with Variety of

NOTES and REMARKS,

Neceſſary to explain and render the whole clear to the meaneſt Capacity,

To which is now added,

A New and accurate LIST of all the Engliſh Regular Lodges in the World, according to their Seniority, with the Dates of each Conſtitution, and Days of Meeting.

By a GENTLEMAN belonging to the Jeruſalem Lodge; a frequent Viſitor at the Queen's Arms, St. Paul's Church-yard; the Horn, in Fleet-ſtreet; Crown and Anchor, Strand; and the Salutation, Newgate-ſtreet.

Try me; prove me.

A NEW EDITION, greatly Enlarged and Improved.

LONDON:

Printed for E. NEWBERY, the Corner of St. Paul's Church-yard; VERNOR and HOOD, Poultry; and CHAMPANTE and WHITROW, Jewry-ſtreet, Aldgate.

1797.

93

I REFACE TO THE FIRST EDITION.

───────────────

TO ALL
F R E E - M A S O N S.

THE Author of the following Pages has the Honour of being well refpected in moft of the Lodges of Reputation in this Metropolis, and has been a frequent Vifitor at the Queen's Arms, St. Paul's Church-yard; the Globe, in Fleet-ftreet; the Jerufalem, at Clerkenwell; Half-moon, Cheapfide; Crown and Anchor in the Strand; Salutation, Grey-Friars; and feveral others of lefs Note.

An Earneft Defire of becoming a perfect Mafter of MASONRY, and the Succefs he met with in his firft Attempt, has rendered him capable of revealing thofe Myfteries to the World, which, till now, have been kept fecret as the Grave.

He acquired his Knowledge at firft from fome loofe Papers belonging to a Merchant to whom he was nearly related, who had been a Member of the Queen's Arms, St. Paul's Church-yard. This Relation dying about ten Years ago, the Editor became poffeffed of his Effects; and on looking over his Papers, among others he found fome Memorandums or Remarks on MASONRY, which excited his Curiofity fo far, that he refolved on accomplifhing his Scheme, without going through the Ceremonies required by the Society.

The Remarks of his Friend abovementioned furnifhed Hints fufficient to make a Trial on an intimate Acquaintance, a FREE MASON, who readily gave him the Sign in the Manner he expected. After a more narrow Infpection on the Part of his Friend, fuch as, where he was made, and when, &c. &c. (to all which he anfwered with great Readinefs) he received an Invitation to fpend an Evening at a Tavern in the Strand, with feveral Acquaintances.

A 2   Elated

Elated by this Succefs, he boldly advanced with his Company; all of whom belonged to the Lodge, and were well known by the TYLER at the Door. After the ufual Ceremony, in which he gave full Satisfaction, he was admitted and took his Seat. That Night he faw two MAKINGS*, and came off full of Spirits.

Soon after he went to another Lodge, where he diftinguifhed himfelf greatly in anfwering the Queftions propofed by the Mafter, which he acquired from his Friend's Manufcripts of the EN-TERED APPRENTICE, and FELLOW-CRAFT's Lectures.

His Regard to the Society, and Refpect to the Public is the only inducement to this Publication, which is intended not only to affift thofe who have been lately made, and ftill remain ignorant of the true Foundation of the Art, but alfo to give all that have an Inclination to become Mafons an Opportunity of confidering the Advantages and Difadvantages of the Engagements and Oaths by which they are bound.—Such is the Intention of this Undertaking; and the Editor flatters himfelf the Brotherhood will not condemn his Officioufnefs in this Refpect, as it will rather ftrengthen than hurt the Intereft of the Society; the Fear of going through the Ceremony, which hitherto has been reprefented in fuch frightful Shapes, being the greateft Obftacle to its future Welfare and Increafe.

The Editor's Ambition is to pleafe; and the Work is fubmitted to the only proper Judges, viz. his Brethren the FREE MASONS; to whom he begs leave to declare, that no private or public Quarrel, the View of Gain, nor any other Motive than the Public Good could ever have induced him to write upon this fubject; and he declares to the World, that the following is the whole of true MASONRY in all its Branches.

---

* *Makings*, the Term ufed in the circular Letters to the Members of the Lodge, acquainting them that New Members are to be admitted the next Lodge Night.

ADVER-

ADVERTISEMENT.

SINCE the former Edition of this Pamphlet was put to Press, the Author has received from his Publisher several anonymous Letters, containing the lowest Abuse and scurrilous Invectives; nay, some have proceeded so far as to threaten his Person. He requests the Favour of all enraged Brethren, who shall chuse to display their Talents for the future, that they will be so kind as to pay the Postage of their Letters, for there can be no Reason why he should put up with their ill Treatment, and pay the Piper into the Bargain. Surely there must be something in this Book very extraordinary; a Something they cannot digest, thus to excite the Wrath and Ire of those hot-brained Mason-bit Gentry! But however unwilling the Editor may be to publish *all* the Letters and Messages he has received on this occasion, yet he cannot be so deficient in returning the Compliment, as to conceal one, which notwithstanding the Threatenings contained in it, appears to be wrote with very little meaning, and he has (sans ceremonie) ventured to publish it verbatim.

For R. S. at Mr. Wm. Nicholls at the Paper Mill St. Paul Church Yard London.

" R S.   London.

" Try thee prove thee * I shall find thee a Scandalous Stinking powcatt, thou pretends to have declared the truth of Masonry to the World. And has Imposed a Lie on the Public Not in one part But in all Parts thou Mentions, I shall meet the in a few Days and will give thee Satisfaction Such a Pike thonk Scandalous Villain Deserves."

The Original of this spirited Letter, with the Post-mark to authenticate it, is left in the hands of Mr. Nicoll, Bookseller, in St. Paul's Church-yard, who has the Editor's leave to shew it to any Gentleman desirous to peruse so pretty an Epistle; and strict Orders are given the Publisher to receive none, for the future, that are not Post-paid.

₊ Those Gentlemen who so often send for JACHIN and BOAZ, and desire the Publisher to tie it up and seal it carefully, to hide it from the Messenger, may safely continue their Commissions, and the Publisher will carefully observe their Order.   R. S.

* Alluding to the Motto in the Title Page, taken from the Fellow Craft's Lecture.

DESCRIPTION *of the* REGALIA *and* EMBLEMATICAL FIGURES *used in* MASONRY, *represented in the* FRONTISPIECE.

1. THE two Pillars called JACHIN and BOAZ, the first signifying *strength*, the second *to establish in the Lord.*
2. The Holy Bible opened, as an Emblem that it should be the Rule of our Faith.
3. The Compass and Square, to square our Actions, and keep them within Bounds, the Master's Emblem or Jewel, which is suspended with a Ribbon round the Neck, and always worn when the Lodge is opened, and on public Days of Meeting, Funerals, &c.
4. The Level, the Senior Warden's Emblem or Jewel.
5. The 24 Inch Gauge, to measure Mason's Work.
6. The Key, the Treasurer's Emblem.

7. The

7. The Sword, prefented to the naked left Breaft of the Apprentice.
8. The Cable, or Rope, put round the Neck of every new-made Mafon at the Time of Making.
9. The Trowel, an Inftrument of great Ufe among Mafons.
10. The Gavel, or fetting Maul, ufed in building Solomon's Temple, the firft Grand Work of Mafonry.
11. The Plumb, Level, Compafs, and Plumb Rule, the Junior Warden's Emblem.
12. The fmall Hammer, to knock off fuperfluous Pieces.
13. The Crofs Pens, the Secretary's Emblem.
14. A Coffin, with a Figure of the maimed body of Hiram (the firft Grand Mafter) painted on it. He was murdered by three Fellow-Crafts, for refufing to reveal the Secret. See p. 31.
15. The Hand Plummet, for taking Perpendiculars.
16. The Sun rifing in the Eaft, emblematical of the Mafter-Mafon, ftanding in the Eaft, and fetting the Men to Work.
17. The Seven Stars, an Aftronomical Emblem, frequently engraved on the Medals worn by Mafons.
18. The Moon, that rules the Night. See p. 14.
19. The Candlefticks, placed in a triangular form.
20. The Columns, ufed by the Senior and Junior Wardens in the Lodge. See p. 37.
21. Two black Rods, carried by the Senior and Junior Deacons.
22. The Three Steps and Pavement.
23. Entrance or Porch to Solomon's Temple.
24. The Terreftrial and Celeftial Globes, reprefenting the Works of Creation.
25. A Machine ufed by Mafons for forming Triangles.
26. The large Rule for meafuring the Work.
27. The three Step Ladder ufed in Mafonry.
28. Hiram's Tent.
29. The White Aprons and Gloves, Emblems of Innocence.
30. Eye of Providence, the Great Superintendent of all the Works of the Univerfe, and Mafonry reprefented as under its immediate Influence.

The Frontifpiece is a Medallion, in Imitation of thofe Medals, or Plates that are common among the Brotherhood. Thefe Medals are ufually of Silver, and fome of them highly finifhed and ornamented, fo as to be worth ten or twenty Guineas. They are fufpended round the Neck with Ribbons of various Colours, and worn on their Public Days of Meeting, at Funeral Proceffions, &c. in Honour of the Craft. On the Reverfe of thefe Medals it is ufual to put the Owner's Coat of Arms, or Cypher, or any other Device that the Owner fancies, and fome even add to the Emblems other Fancy Things that bear fome Analogy to Mafonry.

The Candlefticks, &c. in many Lodges are curioufly wrought, the Chair in which the Grand Mafter fits, as well as thofe of the Mafters of inferior Lodges, are richly carved with Emblematical Figures; their Aprons are bound with Ribbons of various Colours; and, in fhort, every Thing belonging to them is finifhed in the moft elegant Tafte.

a   AN

A N

AUTHENTIC KEY

TO THE DOOR OF

FREE-MASONRY.

THE Origin * of the Society called Free-Mafons is faid by fome to have been a certain Number of Perfons who formed a Refolution to rebuild the Temple of *Solomon* †. This appears from the Lecture, or rather Hiftory, of the Order, at the Making or Raifing of a Member to the Degree of Mafter; which is fully defcribed in the following Work. But I am inclined to think,

* The Rife of this Science (fays an original Record) was before the Flood. In the 4th Chapter of Genefis it is faid, There was a Man named *Lamech* who had two Wives named *Adah* and *Zillah*; by *Adah* he begat two Sons, *Jabal* and *Jubal*; by *Zillah* he begat one Son, called *Tubal Cain*, and a Daughter named *Naamah*. Thefe children found out the Beginning of all the Crafts in the World; *Jabal* found out Geometry; he divided Flocks of Sheep, and built the firft Houfe of Timber and Stone. *Jubal* found out the Art of Mufic, and was the Father of all thofe who handled the Harp. *Tubal Cain* was the Inftructor of all Artificers in Iron and Brafs; and his Daughter difcovered the Craft of Weaving.

† By an old Record it appears, that King *Solomon* confirmed all the Charges which King *David* had given to Mafons in *Jerufalem*; and that the Temple was finifhed, A. M. 3000. In the Year 43, after *Chrift*, Mafons firft came into *England*, and built the Monaftery of *Glaftonbury* in *Somerfetfhire*.

that

(2)

that the chief Defign of the Eftablifhment is to rectify the Heart, inform the Mind, and promote the Moral and Social Virtues of Humanity, Decency, and good Order, as much as poffible in the World : and fome of the Emblems of Free-Mafons confirm this Opinion, fuch as the Compafs, Rule, Square, &c.

In all Countries where Mafonry is practifed, or eftablifhed at this time, there is a Grand Mafter ; but formerly there was only one Grand Mafter, and he was an *Englifhman*. HIS ROYAL HIGHNESS GEORGE PRINCE OF WALES is the Perfon on whom the Dignity is now beftowed, who governs all the Lodges in *Great Britain*, and has the power of delivering the Conftitutions and Laws of the Society to the Mafters who prefide over the fubordinate Affemblies : which Conftitutions muft always be figned by the Grand Secretary of the Order.——The Grand Mafter can hold a Meeting or Lodge when he thinks proper, which is generally the fecond *Saturday* in every Month in the Summer, but oftener in the Winter.

The other Lodges meet regularly twice a Month in the Winter Half-Year, and once a Month in the Summer ; and the Members of each Lodge pay Quarterly, from 3s. 6d. to 5s. into the Hands of the Treafurer ; and this generally defrays the Expence of their Meetings.

There are alfo Quarterly Communications or Meetings, held, at which are prefent the Mafter and Wardens of every Regular Conftitution in and near *London*, where the feveral Lodges fend, by the faid Wardens, different Sums of Money to be paid into the Hands of the Treafurer General, and appropriated to fuch charitable Ufes as the Grand Mafter, and the Mafters of the different Lodges under him, think proper ; but thefe Charities are chiefly confined to Mafons only. Such as have good Recommendations as to their Behaviour and Character, will be affifted with Five, Ten, or Twenty Pounds ; and lefs Sums are diftributed to the indigent Brethren, in Proportion to their Wants, and the Number of Years they have been Members. At thefe Quarterly Communications, large Sums are likewife fent from Lodges in the moft remote Parts of the World, viz. in the *Eaft* and *Weft Indies*, and Accounts tranfmitted of the growth of Mafonry there. The State of the Funds of the Society are likewife communicated to the Company, and the Deliberations of the Meeting taken down by the Secretary, who lays them before the Grand Mafter at the yearly Meeting.

The Number of Members which compofe a Lodge is indeterminate ; but it is no Lodge except there are prefent one Mafter, three Fellow-Crafts, and two Apprentices.

When

(3)

When a Lodge is met, there are two principal Officers under the Master, called Senior and Junior Wardens, whose Business it is to see the Laws of the Society strictly adhered to, and the Word of Command given by the Grand Master regularly followed.

It must be remarked, that the Authority of a Master, though Chief of the Lodge, reaches no farther than he is himself an Observer of the Laws; should he infringe them, the Brethren never fail to censure him; and if this has no Effect, they have a Power of deposing him, on appealing to the Grand Master, and giving their Reasons for it; but they seldom proceed to this Extremity.

As no Doubt the Reader chuses to be made acquainted with every Circumstance of the Ceremony of making a Mason, I shall begin with the following Directions, and proceed regularly in the Description of what further concerns Masonry.

A Man desirous of becoming a Free Mason, should endeavour to get acquainted with a Member of some good Lodge, who will propose him as a Candidate for Admission the next Lodge-Night. The Brother who proposes a New Member, is likewise obliged to inform the Brethren of the Qualifications of the Candidate *. Upon this it is debated whether or not he shall be admitted; and it being carried in the Affirmative, the next Step is to go with the proposer the ensuing Lodge-Night.

The Evening being come when a Lodge is to be held, which generally begins about Seven in the Winter, and Nine in the Summer, as previous Notices are sent to the Members for this Purpose; the Masons are punctual to Time, and it frequently happens, that, in half an Hour, the whole Lodge, to the Number of Fifty or Sixty, are assembled.

The Master, the two Assistants, Secretary, and Treasurer, begin with putting over their Necks a blue Ribbon of a triangular Shape; to the Master's Ribbon hangs a Rule and Compass, which is in some Lodges made of Gold, though in others only gilt: the Assistants, Senior Wardens, and the other Officers, carry the Compass alone.

The Candles are placed upon the Table in the Form of a Triangle; and in the best Lodges the Candlesticks are finely carved with emblematical Figures. Every Brother has an Apron made of white Skin, and the Strings are also of Skin; though some of them chuse to ornament them with Ribbons

---

* For the Good of this, and all other Societies, it were to be wished a more strict Regard was paid, on the Part of the Proposers, to the Character and Morals of every Candidate.

B   of

(4)

of various Colours. On the Grand Days, such as Quarterly Communications, or General Meetings, the Grand Officers Aprons are finely decorated, and they carry the Rule and Compass, the Emblems of the Order.

When they sit down to the Table, the Master's Place is on the East Side, the Bible being opened before him, with the Compass laid thereon, and the Points of them covered with a Lignum Vitæ or Box Square; and the Senior and Junior Wardens opposite to him on the West and South. On the Table is likewise Wine, Punch, &c. to regale the Brethren, who take their Places according to their Seniority. Being thus seated, after a few Minutes, the Master proceeds to * *Open the Lodge* in the following Manner:

Manner of Opening a Lodge, and setting the Men to Work.

Master, to the Junior Deacon. What is the chief Care of a Mason?

Ans. To see that the Lodge is tyled.

Mas. Pray do your duty.

[The Junior Deacon gives Three Knocks at the Door; and the † Tyler on the other Side of the Door answereth, by giving Three Knocks. Then the Junior Deacon tells the Master, saying]

Ans. Worshipful, the Lodge is tyled.

Master, to the Junior Deacon. Pray where is the Junior Deacon's Place in the Lodge?

Deacon's Ans. At the Back of the Senior Warden; or at his Right-Hand, if he permits him.

Mas. Your Business there?

Ans. To carry Messages from the Senior to the Junior Warden, so that they may be dispersed round the Lodge.

Master, to the Senior Deacon. Pray where is the Senior Deacon's Place in the Lodge?

Senior Deacon's Ans. At the Back of the Master; or at his Right-Hand if he permits.

Mas. Your Business there?

Ans. To carry Messages from the Master to the Senior Warden.

Mas. The Junior Warden's Place in the Lodge?

Deacon's Ans. In the South.

* To *open a Lodge,* in Masonry, signifies that it is allowed to speak freely among one another of the Mysteries of the Order.

† A Tyler is properly no more than a Guard, or Centinel placed at the Lodge Door, to give the Sign when any one craves Admittance, that the Wardens may come out and examine him; but he is always one of the Brethren.

2   *Master.*

(5)

Master, to the Junior Warden. Why in the South?

Junior Warden's Anf. The better to obferve the Sun at high Meridian, to call the Men off from Work to Refrefhment, and to fee that they come on in due Time, that the Mafter may have Pleafure and Profit thereby.

Maf. Where is the Senior Warden's Place in the Lodge?

Junior Warden's Anf. In the Weft.

Mafter, to the Senior Warden. Your Bufinefs there, Brother?

Senior Warden's Anfwer. As the Sun fets in the Weft to clofe the Day, fo the Senior Warden ftands in the Weft to clofe the Lodge, to pay the Men their Wages, and difmifs them from their Labour.

Maf. The Mafter's Place in the Lodge?

Senior Warden's Anf. In the Eaft.

Maf. His Bufinefs there?

Senior Warden's Anf. As the Sun rifeth in the Eaft to open the Day, fo the Mafter ftands in the Eaft to open his Lodge, and fet the Men to work.

[Then the Mafter takes off his Hat, and declares the Lodge open as follows]

Mafter. " This Lodge is open, in the Name of Holy
" St. John, forbidding all Curfing, Swearing, or Whifper-
" ing, and all prophane Difcourfe whatever, under no lefs
" Penalty than what the Majority fhall think proper."

The Mafter gives three Knocks upon the Table with a wooden Hammer, and puts on his Hat, the Brethren being uncovered: He then afks, if the Gentleman propofed laft Lodge-Night is ready to be made? and on being anfwered in the Affirmative, he orders the Wardens to go out and prepare the Perfon, who is generally waiting in a Room at fome Diftance from the Lodge Room by himfelf, being left there by his Friend who propofed him. He is conducted into another Room, which is totally dark; and then afked, Whether he is confcious of having the Vocation neceffary to be received? On anfwering Yes, he is afked his Name, Surname, and Profeffion. When he has anfwered thefe Queftions, whatever he has about him made of Metal is taken away, as Buckles, Buttons, Rings, &c. and even the Money in his Pocket*. Then they uncover his Right Knee, and put his Left Foot with his Shoe on into a Slipper †; hoodwink him with a Handkerchief, and leave him to his Re-

* In fome Lodges they are fo particular, that the Candidate's Clothes are taken off, if there be Lace on them.
† This is not practifed in every Lodge; fome only flipping the Heel of the Shoe down.

B 2

flection

flection for about Half an Hour. The Chamber is alſo guarded within and without by ſome of the Brethren who have drawn Swords in their Hands. The Perſon who pro-pſed the Candidate ſtays in the Room with him ; but they are not permitted to converſe together.

During this Silence, and while the Candidate is preparing, the Brethren in the Lodge are putting every Thing in order for his Reception there ; ſuch as drawing the annexed Figure on the Floor at the upper Part of the Room ; which is ge-nerally done with Chalk and Charcoal intermixed ; though ſome Lodges uſe Tape and little Nails to form it ; which prevents any Mark or Stain on the Floor. It is drawn Eaſt and Weſt. The Maſter ſtands in the Eaſt, with the Square hanging at his Breaſt, the Holy Bible opened at the Goſpel of St. *John*, and three lighted Tapers are placed in the Form of a Triangle in the Midſt of the Drawing on the Floor.

The Propoſer then goes and knocks three Times at the Door of the Grand Apartment, in which the Ceremony is to be performed. The Maſter anſwers within by three Strokes with the Hammer, and the Junior Warden aſks, Who comes there ? The Candidate anſwers (after another who piompts him) "One who begs to receive Part of the Benefit of this "Right Worſhipful Lodge, dedicated to St. *John*, as many "Brothers and Fellows have done before me." The Doors are then opened, and the Senior and Junior Wardens, or their Aſſiſtants, receive him, one on the Right, and the other on the Left, and conduct him blindfolded Three Times * round the Drawing on the Floor, and bring him up to the Foot of it, with his Face to the Maſter †, the Brethren ranging themſelves on each Side, and making a confuſed Noiſe, by ſtriking on the Attributes of the Order, which they carry in their Hands ‡.

---

* In ſome Lodges the Candidates are led Nine Times round ; but as this is very tireſome to the Perſon who is to undergo the Operation, his Pa-tience being pretty well tired by being blinded ſo long beforehand, it is very juſtly omitted.

† Many Lodges throw a fine Powder, or Roſin on the Floor, which with the Illumination of the Room, has a pretty Effect.

‡ This Cuſtom is not obſerved in all Lodges.

PLAN

PLAN *of the* DRAWING *on the* FLOOR *at the making of a* MASON.

EXPLANATION.

A Senior Deacon, with a black Rod.
B Paſt-Maſter, with the Sun and Compaſſes, and a String of Cords.
C Senior Warden, with the Level, and a Column in his Hand.
D Junior Deacon, with a black Rod.
E Junior Warden, with a Column in his Hand.
F The Secretary, with Croſs Pens.
G H I Candles.
✻ Maſons ſtanding round at the Ceremony.

When

(8)

When this Part of the Ceremony is ended, the Master who stands at the upper End, facing the Foot or Steps of the Drawing on the Floor, behind a low Arm-chair, asks the following Question, Whether you have a desire to become a Mason? and if it is of your own free Will and Choice? Upon which the Candidate answers, Yes. "Let him see "the Light," says the Master: They then take the Hand-kerchief from his Eyes, and whilst they are so doing, the Brethren form a Circle round him, with their Swords drawn in their Hands, the Points of which are presented to his Breast. The Ornaments borne by the Officers, the glit-tering of the Swords, and fantastic Appearance of the Bre-thren in White Aprons, creates great Surprise, especially to a Person, who for above an Hour has been fatigued with the Bandage over his Eyes; and his Uncertainty concerning what is further to be done for his Reception, must, no Doubt, throw his Mind into great Perplexity *,

The Candidate is then directed to advance Three Times to a Stool at the Foot of the Arm-chair; he is taught to step in a proper Manner by one of the Assistants. Upon the Stool are placed the Rule and Compass; and one of the Brethren says to the Candidate to this Effect: "You are "now entering into a respectable Society, which is more "serious and important than you imagine. It admits of "nothing contrary to Law, Religion, or Morality; nor "does it allow any Thing inconsistent with the Allegiance "due to His Majesty; the Worshipful Grand Master will "inform you the rest †."

As soon as the Speaker has ended his Speech, he is de-sired to put his Right Knee upon the Stool, which is bare, as mentioned above ‡, and his left foot is put into a Slipper, with the Shoe on, or the Shoe slipped at the Heel, to repre-sent a Slipper.

The Candidate being in this Posture, the Worshipful Grand Master addresses him to the following Effect: "Do "you promise never to tell, write, or disclose, in any man-"ner whatever, the Secrets of Free Masonry and Free Ma-

* The ancient Masons made use of a Prayer inserted in the Apprentice's Lecture; but the Moderns leave it out when they make a Brother.

† It is here to be understood, that in different Lodges this Speech varies: as also do the Forms of Making in some Respects, which may be seen in the Entered Apprentice's Lecture; where the only proper and ancient Method is clearly pointed out.

‡ The ancient Custom was thus: The Candidate, though kneeling on his Right Knee, should have his Left Foot in the Air; but this Position being fatiguing, it is omitted in most Lodges.

"sons,

(9)

" fons, except to a Brother at the Lodge, and in the Pre-
" fence of the Worfhipful Grand Mafter?" On which the
Perfon fays, " I do." His Waiftcoat is then unbottoned *,
and the Point of a Pair of Compaffes † placed upon his
naked Left Breaft, and he himfelf holds it with his Left
Hand, his Right Hand being laid upon the Gofpel opened at
St. *John*; when the following Oath is adminiftered to him,
he repeating it after the Mafter :

THE OATH.

" I——A. B. of my own Free Will and Accord, and in
" the Prefence of Almighty God ‡, and this Right Wor-
" fhipful Lodge, dedicated to St. *John*, do hereby, and herein
" moft folemnly and fincerely fwear, that I will a ways
" hale, conceal, and never reveal any of the Secrets or
" Myfteries of Free Mafonry, that fhall be delivered to me
" now, or at any Time hereafter, except it be to a true and
" lawful Brother, or in a juft and lawful Lodge of Brothers
" and Fellows, him or them whom I fhall find to be fuch,
" after juft Trial and due Examination. I furthermore do
" fwear that I will not write it, print it, cut it, paint it,
" ftain it, mark it, ftain or engrave it, or caufe it fo to be
" done, upon any thing moveable or immoveable under the
" Canopy of Heaven, whereby it may become legible or
" intelligible, or the leaft Appearance of the Character of a
" Letter, whereby the fecret Art may be unlawfully obtained:
" All this I fwear, with a ftrong and fteady Refolution to
" perform the fame, without any Hefitation, mental Refer-
" vation, or Self-evafion of Mind in me whatfoever; under
" no lefs penalty than to have my Throat cut acrofs, my
" Tongue torn out by the Root, and that it be buried in
" the Sands of the Sea, at Low Water Mark, a Cable's
" Length from the Shore, where the Tide ebbs and flows
" twice in twenty-four Hours. So help me God, and
" keep me ftedfaft in this my Entered Apprentice's Obliga-
" tion." [*He kiffes the Book.*]
    The now made Member is then taught the Sign, Grip,
and Pafs-word of the Entered Apprentice, which will be

---

* This is done laft a Woman fhould offer hr felf. If we believe the
Irifh, there is a dy at this Time in *Ireland*, who has gone through the
whole Ceremony, and is as good a Mafon as any of them.
    † The Ancients ufed a Sword or Spear inftead of a Compafs:
    ‡ The Form of the Oath differs in many Lodges, though this is the
ftricteft in Ufe; and in fome Societies inftead of faying, " In the Prefence
" of Almighty God," it runs thus, " I promife before the Great Architect
" of the Univerfe," &c.

                                                                                    feen

106

(10)

feen more clearly in the following Lecture belonging to that Part of Mafonry.

He is alfo learnt the Step, or how to advance to the Maf-ter upon the Drawing on the Floor, which in fome Lodges refembles the Grand Building, termed a Mofaic Palace, and is defcribed with the utmoft Exactnefs. They alfo draw other Figures, one of which is called the Laced Tuft, and the other, the Throne befet with Stars. There is alfo re-prefented a perpendicular Line in the Form of a Mafon's In-ftrument, commonly called the Plumb-Line; and another Figure which reprefents the Tomb of *Hiram*, the firft Grand Mafter, who has been dead almoft Three Thoufand Years. Thefe are all explained to him in the moft accurate Manner; and the Ornaments or Emblems of the Order are defcribed with great Facility. The Ceremony being now ended, the new-made Member is obliged to take a Mop out of a Pail of Water brought for that Purpofe, and rub out the Drawing on the Floor, if it is done with Chalk and Charcoal. Then he is conducted back, and every Thing that he was divefted of is reftored, and he takes his Seat on the Right Hand of the Mafter. He alfo receives an Apron, which he puts on; and the Lift of the Lodges is likewife given him.

The Brethren now congratulate the new-made Member, and all return to the Table to regale themfelves; when the Mafter propofes a Health to the young Brother, which is drank with the greateft Applaufe by the whole Body, the new Mafon fitting all the while. After which he, inftructed by a Brother, takes a Bumper, and drinks " To the Wor-" fhipful Grand Mafter, the Senior and Junior Wardens, " the reft of the Officers and Members of the Lodge, wifh-" ing them Succefs in all their public and private Under-" takings, to Mafonry in general, and that Lodge in par-" ticular, craving their Affiftance." To which they anfwer, " they will affift him." And after he has drank, he throws his Glafs from him, and brings it back three Times, and then fets it down on the Table, the reft doing the fame in exact Order. This they call Firing: Then they clap their Hands Nine Times divided into Three, and ftop between each, keeping true Time.

The Reader having been led thus far, it is high Time to introduce the Apprentice's Lecture, which is intended not only to amufe, but likewife to inftruct him in the Part he is entered into. The readinefs of many of the Brethren in anfwering the Queftions, adds a Luftre to the Order, the Members vying with each other who fhall moft contribute to the Edification of their new Brother.

The

(11)

The Entered Apprentice's Lecture.

Maf. BROTHER, is there any Thing between you and me? *Anf.* There is, Right Worfhipful.

Maf. What is it Brother, pray? *Anf.* A Secret.

Maf. What is that Secret, Brother? *Anf.* Mafonry.

Maf. Then I prefume you are a Mafon?

Anf. I am fo taken and accepted amongft Brothers and Fellows.

Maf. Pray what fort of a Man ought a Mafon to be?

Anf. A Man that is born of a Free Woman.

Maf. Where was you firft prepared to be made a Mafon?

Anf. In my Heart.

Maf. Where was you next prepared?

Anf. In a Room adjoining to the Lodge.

Maf. How was you prepared, Brother?

Anf. I was neither naked, nor clothed, bare-foot, nor fhod; deprived of all Metal; hood-winked, with a Cable Tow about my Neck, where I was led to the Door of the Lodge, in a halting moving Pofture, by the Hand of a Friend, whom I afterwards found to be a Brother.

Maf. How do you know it to be a Door, you being blinded?

Anf. By finding a Stoppage, and afterwards an Entrance, or Admittance.

Maf. How got you Admittance?

Anf. By three Knocks.

Maf. What was faid to you within?

Anf. Who comes there?

Maf. Your Anfwer, Brother?

Anf. One who begs to have and receive Part of the Benefit of this Right Worfhipful Lodge, dedicated to St. *John*, as many Brothers and Fellows have done before me.

Maf. How do you expect to obtain it?

Anf. By being free born, and well reported.

Maf. What was faid to you then? *Anf.* Enter.

Maf. How did you enter, and upon what?

Anf. Upon the Point of a Sword or Spear, or fome warlike Inftrument prefented to my naked left Breaft.

Maf. What was faid to you then?

Anf. I was afked if I felt any thing.

Maf. What was your Anfwer?

* The Reader is defired to obferve, that here I give the *Whole* of the Lectures, as delivered in the primitive Time; but the modern Mafons leave out at leaft one-half.

C *Anf.* I did,

(12)

Anf. I did, but I could fee nothing.

Maf. You have told me how you was received; pray who received you? *Anf.* The Junior Warden.

Maf. How did he difpofe of you?

Anf. He delivered me to the Mafter, who ordered me to kneel down and receive the Benefit of a Prayer.

Brethren, let us Pray.

O LORD God, thou great and univerfal Mafon of the World, and firft Buil of Man, as it were a Temple; be with us, O Lord, as thou haft promifed, when two or three are gathered together in thy Name, thou wilt be in the midft of them : Be with us, O Lord, and blefs all our Undertakings, and grant that this our Friend may become a faithful Brother. Let Grace and Peace be multiplied unto him, through the Knowledge of our Lord Jefus Chrift; And grant, O Lord, as he putteth forth his Hand to thy Holy Word, that he may alfo put forth his Hand to ferve a Brother, but not to hurt himfelf or his Family ; that whereby may be given to us great and precious Promifes, that by this we may be Partakers of thy Divine Nature, having efcaped the Corruption that is in the World through Luft.

O Lord God, add to our Faith Virtue, and to Virtue Knowledge, and to Knowledge Temperance, and to Temperance Prudence, and to Prudence Patience, and to Patience Godlinefs, and to Godlinefs Brotherly Love, and to Brotherly Love Charity; and grant, O Lord, that Mafonry may be bleffed throughout the World, and thy Peace be upon us, O Lord, and grant that we may be all united as one, through our Lord Jefus Chrift, who liveth and reigneth for ever and ever. *Amen.*

Maf. After this Prayer, what was faid to you?

Anf. I was afked who I put my Truft in?

Maf. Your Anfwer, Brother? *An* In God.

Maf. What was the next Thing faid o you?

Anf. I was taken by the Right Hand, and a Brother faid, Rife up, and follow your Leader, and fear no Danger.

Maf. After all this, how was you difpofed of?

Anf. I was led three Times round the Lodge.

Maf. Where did you meet with the firft Oppofition?

Anf. At the Back of the Junior Warden in the South, where I gave the fame Three Knocks as at the Door?

Maf. What Anfwer did he give you ?

Anf. He faid, Who comes there ?

4   *Maf.*

Maf. Your Anfwer?

Anf. The fame as at the Door, One who begs to have and receive, &c.

Maf. Where did you meet with the fecond Oppofition?

Anf. At the Back of the Senior Warden in the Weft, where I made the fame Repetition as at the Door. He faid, Who comes here? One who begs to have and receive, &c.

Maf Where did you meet with the third Oppofition?

Anf. At the Back of the Mafter in the Eaft, where I made the Repetition as before.

Maf. What did the Mafter do with you?

Anf. He ordered me back to the Senior Warden in the Weft to receive Inftructions.

Maf. What where the Inftructions he gave you.

Anf. He taught me to take one Step upon the firft Step of a right Angle oblong Square, with my left Knee bare bent, my Body upright, my right Foot forming a Square, my naked Right Hand upon the Holy Bible, with the Square and Compafs thereon; my left Hand fupporting the fame; where I took that folemn Obligation or Oath of a Mafon.

Maf. Brother, can you repeat that Obligation?

Anf. I will do my Endeavour, with your Affiftance, Worfhipful.

Maf. Stand up and begin.

[Here the Oath is repeated, as mentioned before. After repeating this Obligation, they drink a Toaft to the Heart that conceals, and to the Tongue that never reveals. The Mafter in the Chair gives it, and they all fay Ditto, and draw the Glaffes acrofs their Throats, as aforefaid.]

Maf. Now, Brother, after you received the Obligation, what was faid to you?

Anf. I was afked what I moft defired.

Maf. What was your Anfwer.

Anf. To be brought to Light.

Maf. Who brought you to Light.

Anf. The Mafter and the reft of the Brethren.

Maf. When you was thus brought to Light, what were the firft Things you faw?

Anf. The Bible, Square, and Compafs.

Maf. What was it they told you they fignified?

Anf. Three great Lights in Mafonry.

Maf. Explain them, Brother?

Anf. The Bible to rule and govern our Faith; the Square to fquare our Actions; the Compafs to keep us within Bounds with all Men, particularly with a Brother.

C 2

Maf.

(14)

Maſ. What where the next Things that were ſhewn to you?

Anſ. Three Candles, which I was told were three leſſer Lights in Maſonry.

Maſ. What do they repreſent?

Anſ. The Sun, Moon, and Maſter-Maſon.

Maſ. Why ſo, Brother?

Anſ. There is the Sun to rule the Day, the Moon to rule the Night, and the Maſter-Maſon his Lodge, or at leaſt ought ſo to do.

Maſ. What was then done to you?

Anſ. The Maſter took me by the Right-Hand, and gave me the Grip and Word of an Entered Apprentice, and ſaid, Riſe, my Brother JACHIN,

> [Sometimes they ſhew you the Sign before the Grip and Word is given, which is JACHIN: It is the Entered Apprentice's Word, and the Grip thereto belonging is to pinch with your Right Thumb Nail upon the firſt Joint of your Brother's Right Hand.]

Maſ. Have you got this Grip and Word, Brother?

Anſ. I have, Right Worſhipful.

Maſ. Give it to your Brother.

> [Then he takes his next Brother by the Right Hand, and gives him the Grip and Word, as before deſcribed.]

The 1ſt Brother gives him the Grip.

The 2d Brother ſays, What's this?

1ſt Bro. The Grip of an Entered Apprentice.

2d Bro. Has it got a Name?   *1ſt Bro.* It has,

2d Bro. Will you give it me?

1ſt Bro. I'll letter it with you, or halve it.

2d Bro. I'll halve it with you.

1ſt Bro. Begin.

2d Bro. No. You begin firſt.

1ſt Bro. JA-

2d Bro. CHIN.

1ſt Bro. JACHIN.

2d Bro. It is right, Worſhipful Maſter.

Maſ. What was the next Thing that was ſhewn to you?

Anſ. The Guard or Sign of an Entered Apprentice*.

Maſ. Have you got the Guard or Sign of an Entered Apprentice?

> [He draws his Right Hand acroſs his Throat (as aforeſaid) to ſhew the Maſter that he has.]

---

* The Guard or Sign as they call it, is by drawing your Right Hand acroſs your Throat edgeways; which is to remind you of the Penalty of your Obligation, that you would ſooner have your Throat cut acroſs than diſcover the Secrets of Maſonry.

Maſ.

(15)

Maf. After this, what was said to you?

Anf. I was ordered to be taken back, and invested with what I had been divested of; and to be brought again to return Thanks, and to receive the Benefit of a Lecture, if Time would permit.

Maf. After what you had been divested of was restored, what was next done to you?

Anf. I was brought to the North West Corner of the Lodge, in order to return Thanks.

Maf. How did you return Thanks?

Anf. I stood in the North West Corner of the Lodge, and, with the Instruction of a Brother, I said, Master, Senior and Junior Wardens, Senior and Junior Deacons, and the rest of the brethren of this Lodge, I return you Thanks for the honour you have done me in making me a Mason, and admitting me a member of this Worthy Society.

Maf. What was then said to you?

Anf. The Master called me up to the North East Corner of the Lodge at his Right Hand.

Maf. Did he present you with any thing?

Anf. He presented me with an Apron, which he put on me: He told me it was a badge of Innocence, more ancient than the Golden Fleece or the *Roman* Eagle; more honoured than the Star and Garter, or any other Order under the Sun, that could be conferred upon me at that Time, or any Time hereafter.

Maf. What were the next Things that were shewn you?

Anf. I was set down by the Master's Right Hand, who shewed me the Working Tools of an Entered Apprentice.

Maf. What were they?

Anf. The 24 Inch Gauge, the Square, and common Gavel or Setting Maul.

Maf. What are their Uses?

Anf. The Square to square my Work, the 24 Inch Gauge to measure my Work, the common Gavel to knock off all superfluous Matter, whereby the Square may fit easy and just.

Maf. Brother, as we are not all working Masons, we apply them to our Morals, which we call spiritualizing: Explain them.

Anf. The 24 Inch Gauge represents the 24 Hours of the Day.

Maf. How do you spend them, Brother?

Anf. Six Hours to work in, six Hours to serve God, and six to serve a Friend or a Brother, as far as lies in my Power, without being detrimental to myself or family.

I come now to the Entered Apprentice's Reasons; but as the ceremony of drinking Healths among the Masons takes up much of their Time, we must stop a little, in order to introduce

(16)

troduce fome of them. The firft is, " To the Heart that
" conceals, and the Tongue that never reveals ;" Then
" The King and Royal Family ;" and, " To all Brethren
" wherefoever difperfed *." The Pleafures they enjoy,
Purity of their Sentiments, and the uniformity that always
reign in their Affemblies, is far from being tirefom' or in-
fipid. I next proceed to the

Entered Apprentice's Reafons †.

Maf. WHY was you neither naked nor clothed, bare-
footed nor fhod, with a Cable-Tow (or Halter)
about your Neck?

Anf. If I had recanted, and ran out in the Street, the People would have faid I was mad ; but if a Brother had feen
me, he would have brought me back, and feen me done Juftice by.

Maf. Why was you hood-winked ?

Anf. That my heart may conceal before my eyes did difcover.

Maf. The fecond Reafon, Brother ?

Anf. As I was in Darknefs at that Time, I fhould keep
all the world in Darknefs.

Maf. Why was you deprived of all Metal ?

Anf. That I fhould bring nothing offenfive or defenfive
in the Lodge.

Maf. Give me the fecond Reafon, Brother ?

Anf. As I was poor and pennylefs when I was made a Mafon, it informed me that I fhould affift all poor and pennylefs
Brethren as far as lay in my Power.

Maf. Brother, you told me you gave three diftinct Knocks
at the Door : Pray what do they fignify ?

Anf. A certain Text in Scripture.

Maf. What is that Text ?

Anf. " Afk, and you fhall have ; Seek, and you fhall find ;
" Knock and it fhall be opened unto you."

Maf. How do you apply this Text in Mafonry ?

Anf. I fought in my Mind ; I afked of my Friend ; I
knocked and the Door of Mafonry became open unto me.

Maf. Why had you a Sword, Spear, or fome other warlike Inftrument prefented to your naked Left Breaft particularly ?

Anf. Becaufe the Left Breaft is the neareft the Heart, that
it might be the more a Prick to my Confcience, as it pricked
my Flefh at that Time.

* Thefe Toafts or Healths are all drank with Three Times Three, which
is performed in a moft regular Manner, and an Huzza at the End of each, as
before defcribed.
† This in fact is only a Continuation of the Lecture.

Mafter.

113

(17)

Maf. Why was you led three Times round the Lodge?

Anf. That all the Brethren might fee I was duly prepared.

Maf. When you was made an Apprentice, why was your
Left Knee bare bent?

Anf. Becaufe tho Left Knee is the weakeft part of my body,
and an Entered Apprentice is the weakeft Part of Mafonry,
into which Degree I was then entering.

[Here the Brethren refume their Glaffes, and drink a
Health fometimes to the Grand Mafter; at other Times
to the Wardens, or other Officers, and then proceed.]

The form af a Lodge.

Maf. BROTHER, pray what makes a Lodge?

    Anf. Right Worfhipful, a certain Number of Ma-
fons met together to work.

Maf. Pray what Number makes a Lodge?

Anf. Three, Five, Seven, or Eleven.

Maf. Why do Three make a Lodge?

Anf. Becaufe there were Three Grand Mafons in the
building of the world, and alfo that noble Piece of Architecture, Man; which are fo complete in Proportion, that
the Ancients began their Architecture by the fame Rules.

Maf. The fecond Reafon, Brother?

Anf. There were three Grand Mafons at the building of
Solomon's Temple.

Maf. Why do Five make a Lodge?

Anf. Becaufe every Man is endowed with Five Senfes.

Maf. What are the Five Senfes?

Anf. Hearing, Seeing, Smelling, Tafting, and Feeling.

Maf. What Ufe are thofe Five Senfes to you in Mafonry?

Anf. Three are of great Ufe to me, *viz.* Hearing, Seeing,
and Feeling.

Maf. What Ufe are they Brother?

Anf. Hearing is to hear the Word; Seeing is to fee the
Sign; Feeling is to feel the Grip, that I may know a Brother as well in the Dark as in the Light.

Maf. Why fhould feven make a Lodge?

Anf. Becaufe there are feven liberal fciences.

Maf. Will you name them, Brother?

Anf. Grammar, Rhetoric, Logic, Arithmetic, Geometry,
Mufic, and Aftronomy.

Maf. Brother, what do thefe Sciences teach you?

Anf. Grammar teaches me the Art of Writing and Speaking the Language taught me according to the firft, fecond,
and third Concord.

Maf. What doth Rhetoric teach you?

Anf. The Art of Speaking upon any Topic whatfoever.

                                         Maf.

Maf. What doth Logic teach you?

Anf. The Art of Reafoning well, whereby you may find out Truth from Falfehood.

Maf. What doth Arithmetic teach you?

Anf. The Ufe of Numbers.

Maf. What doth Geometry teach you?

Anf. The Art of Meafuring, whereby the *Egyptians* found out their own Land, or the fame quantity which they had before the overflowing of the River *Nile*, that frequently ufed to water their Country, at which time they fled to the Mountains till it went c— again, and this made them have continual Quarrels about their Lands.

Maf. What doth Mufic teach you, Brother?

Anf. The Virtue of Sounds.

Maf. What doth Aftronomy teach you?

Anf. The Knowledge of the Heavenly Bodies.

Maf. Why fhould Eleven make a Lodge, Brother?

Anf. There were Eleven *Patriarchs* when *Jofeph* was fold into *Egypt*, and fuppofed to be loft.

Maf. The fecond Reafon, Brother?

Anf. There were but Eleven Apoftles when *Judas* betrayed Chrift.

Maf. What Form is your Lodge?

Anf. An oblong Square.

Maf. How long, Brother?

Anf. From Eaft to Weft.

Maf. How wide, Brother?

Anf. Between North and South?

Maf. How high, Brother?

Anf. From the Earth to the Heavens.

Maf. How deep, Brother?

Anf. From the Surface of the Earth to the Centre.

Maf. Why is your Lodge faid to be from the Surface to the Centre of the Earth?

Anf. Becaufe that Mafonry is univerfal.

Maf. Why is your Lodge fituate Eaft and Weft?

Anf. Becaufe all Churches or Chapels are or ought to be fo.

Maf. Why fo, Brother?

Anf. Becaufe the Gofpel was firft preached in the Eaft, and extended itfelf to the Weft.

Maf. What fupports your Lodge?

Anf. Three great Pillars.

Maf. What are their Names?

Anf. Wifdom, Strength, and Beauty.

Maf. Who doth the Pillar of Wifdom reprefent?

Anf. The Mafter in the Eaft.

Maf. Who doth the Pillar of Beauty reprefent?

Anf.

Anf. The Junior Warden in the South.

Maf. Why fhould the Mafter reprefent the Pillar of Wifdom ?

Anf. Becaufe he gives Inftructions to the Crafts to carry on their work in a proper manner, with good Harmony.

Maf. Why fhould the Senior Warden reprefent the Pillar of Strength?

Anf. As the Sun fets to finifh the Day, fo the Senior Warden ftands in the Weft to pay the Hirelings their Wages, which is the Strength and Support of all Bufinefs.

Maf. Why fhould the Junior Warden reprefent the Pillar of Beauty?

Anf. Becaufe he ftands in the South at high Twelve at Noon, which is the Beauty of the Day, to call the Men off from Work to Refrefhment, and to fee that they come on again in due time, that the Mafter may have Pleafure and Profit therein.

Maf. Why is it faid that your Lodge is fupported by thofe three great Pillars, Wifdom, Strength, and Beauty ?

Anf. Becaufe Wifdom, Strength, and Beauty is the Finifher of all Works, and nothing can be carried on without them.

Maf. Why fo, Brother?

Anf. Becaufe there is Wifdom to contrive, Strength to fupport, and Beauty to adorn.

Maf. Had you any Covering to your Lodge ?

Anf. Yes, a clouded Canopy of divers Colours.

Maf. How blows a Mafon's Wind, Brother ?

Anf. Due Eaft and Weft.

Maf. What is it o'Clock, Brother ?   *Anf.* High Twelve.

Maf. Call the Men off from Work to Refrefhment, and fee that they come on again in due Time.

[The Entered Apprentice's Lecture being finifhed, it is cuftomary for the Mafter to call upon one of the Brethren, who can beft acquit himfelf, for the following Song, which is always readily complied with.]

SONG, *At the Conclufion of the Entered Apprentice's* LECTURE.

    COME, let us prepare,
      We Brothers that are,
Affembled on every Occafion ;
   Let us drink, laugh, and fing,
   Our Wine has a Spring ;
Here's a Health to an Accepted Mafon
           Chorus. Let's drink, &c.

   The world is in Pain,
   Our Secrets to gain,
And ftill let them wonder and gaze on !

          D   They

(20)

They ne'er can divine,
The Word or the Sign
Of a free and an Accepted Mason.
 'Tis this, and 'tis that,
 They cannot tell what,
Why so many great Men of the Nation,
 Should Aprons put on,
 To make themselves one,
With a Free and an accepted Mason.
 Great Kings, Dukes, and Lords,
 Have laid by their Swords,
Our Myst'ry to put a good Grace on;
 And ne'er been asham'd
 To hear themselves nam'd,
With a Free and an Accepted Mason.
 Antiquity's Pride,
 We have on our side,
And it maketh Men just in their Station;
 There's nought but what's good,
 To be understood,
By a Free and an Accepted Mason.
 We're true and sincere,
 And just to the Fair,
Who will trust us on every Occasion;
 No mortal can more
 The Ladies adore,
Than a Free and an Accepted Mason.
 Then join Hand and Hand,
 T'each other firm stand,
Let's be merry, and put a bright Face on;
 What Mortal can boast,
 So noble a Toast,
As a Free and an Accepted Mason?

While this Song is singing, they all stand round the Table,
and when they come to the last Verse they join Hands cross-
ways in the following Manner: The Right Hand Man
takes hold of the Left Hand of his Neighbour with his Right
Hand; and the Left Hand Man takes hold of the Right
Hand of his next Brother with his Left Hand, so as to form
a Chain by so many Links, and all join in the Chorus,
jumping violently with their Feet on the Floor, and shaking
their Hands up and down, linked together as above, keeping
exact time with both.

Every one now talks of what he pleases; and as it is generally
half an Hour before they proceed to Business, those who perhaps have ordered a Supper retire into another Room; but before

117

(21)

fore they are permitted, the Mafter proceeds *to call the Men off from work*, as it is termed, which is done in this Manner: The Mafter whifpers to the Senior Deacon, who fits on his Right Hand, and fays, "It is high time to call the men from Work to refrefh themfelves:" The Senior Deacon whifpers it to the Senior Warden ; and it is communicated from him to the Junior Deacon, who carries it to the Junior Warden ; he proclaims it openly to the Lodge, and fets his Column upright*, and the Senior Warden lays his down, which fignifies that the Junior Warden is intrufted with the C e of the Lodge, while the Brethren refrefh themfelves.

In this place it will be neceffary to acquaint the Reader how he may difcover an Entered Apprentice by drinking with him in company. Take the Glafs with your Right Hand, and draw it acrofs your Throat, either before or after you drink ; and if an Apprentice is prefent, he will immediately take Notice of it, by afking you fome Queftion in Mafonry, which you will readily anfwer from this Book. If he afks you the meaning of your doing that, you may whifper to him, that it is the Penalty of the Obligation of an Entered Apprentice. From this Anfwer he will proceed farther in his inquiry.

The Brethren having now regaled themfelves, they take their Seats, and the Mafter proceeds to fet them on again, which is performed in the fame manner as the calling off ; with this Difference, the Warden proclaims, "It is our "Worfhipful Mafter's Pleafure that this Lodge is called "from Refrefhment to Work." The Junior Warden lays down his Column, and the Senior fets his up. But as it often happens that the Time will not permit for the Fellow-Craft's Lecture, they clofe the Lodge, which is done after the fame Manner as that of opening. The Senior Warden declares it in the following Words: "It is our Mafter's "Will and Pleafure, that this Lodge ftand clofed till the "Firft or Third Wednefday in the next Month," according to the Night the Lodge is held. Then the Mafter, Wardens, Deacons, Secretary, &c. take off the Enfigns and Ornaments from their necks, and every one is at Liberty to depart or ftay longer ; every thing of Mafonry is excluded ; they talk of what they pleafe, and fing various Songs for their Amufement.

I fhall now proceed to the Second Degree of Mafonry, called the *Fellow Craft's*: that is, one who has ferved his Time juftly and lawfully as an Entered Apprentice, and defires to

---

* The Senior and Junior Warden's Columns are about twenty-five Inches long, and reprefent the Columns that fupport the Porch of *Solomon's* Temple; The Senior's is called JACHIN, and fignifies *Strength*; the Junior's BOAZ, and fignifies, *to eftablifh in the Lord*. See the Firft Book of Kings, Chap. VII.

D 2

become

118

(22)

become more perfect in Masonry, by being admitted a Fellow Craft. But in most Lodges at this Time, they are made Entered Apprentices and Fellow Craft the same Evening. The Ceremony is the same, though they have different Lectures, Pass-Word, and Grip belonging to each.

The Fellow-Craft's Lecture.

Maf. BROTHER, are you a Fellow-Craft?
 Anf. I am. Try me, prove me.
Maf. Where was you made a Fellow-Craft?
Anf. In a just and lawful Lodge.
Maf. How was you prepared to be made a Fellow-Craft?
Anf. I was neither naked nor cloathed, bare-foot, nor shod; in a halting moving Posture; deprived of all Metal, I was led to the Door of the Lodge by the Hand of a Brother.
Maf. How got you Admittance?
Anf. By three distinct Knocks.
Maf. What was said to you within?
Anf. Who comes there?
Maf. Your Answer, Brother?
Anf. One who has served his Time justly and lawfully as an Entered Apprentice, and now begs to become more perfect in Masonry, by being admitted a Fellow-Craft.
Maf. How do you expect to attain to this Degree?
Anf. By the Benefit of a Pass-Word.
Maf. Have you got that Pass-word?
Anf. I have.
Maf. Give it me, Brother?
Anf. SHIBBOLETH*.
Maf. What did he then say to you?
Anf. Pass, *Shibboleth.*
Maf. What became of you then?
Anf. I was led twice round the Lodge.
Maf. Where did you meet with the first Opposition?
Anf. At the Back of the Senior Warden.
Maf. Where did you meet with the Second Opposition?
Anf. At the Back of the Master, where I repeated the same as before.
Maf. What did he do with you?
Anf. He ordered me back to the Senior Warden to receive Instructions.
Maf. What Instructions did he give you?
Anf. He taught me to shew the Master my due Guard, and to take two Steps upon the second Step of a Right Angled Oblong Square, with my Right Knee bent bare, my

* SHIBBOLETH, the Pass-word of a Fellow-Craft; signifies *Plenty.* See the xiith Chapter of the Book of Judges.

2

Left

(23)

Left Foot forming a Square, my Body upright, my Right Hand on the Holy Bible, my left Arm fupported by the Points of the Compaffes, forming a Square, where I took the Obligation of a Fellow-Craft.

Maf. Have you got that Obligation, Brother?

Anf. I have, Right Worfhipful.

Maf. Can you repeat it ?

Anf. I'll do my Endeavour, Right Worfhipful, with your Affiftance.

Maf. Pray ftand up, and let the Brethren hear it.

The Obligation of a Fellow-craft

" I——*A. B.* of my own Free Will and Accord, and in
" the Prefence of Almighty God, and this Right Worfhipful
" Lodge, dedicated to St. *John*, do hereby fwear, that I
" will always hale, conceal, and never reveal, that Part of
" a Fellow-Craft to an Entered Apprentice, or either of
" them, except it be in a true and lawful Lodge of Crafts,
" him or them whom I fhall find to be fuch, after juft Trial
" and Examination.——I do furthermore fwear, that I will
" anfwer all Signs and Summonfes fent to me from a Lodge
" of Crafts, within the Length of a Cable-Tow*. I alfo
" fwear, that I will not wrong a Brother, nor fee him
" wronged, but give him timely Notice of all approaching
" Dangers whatfoever, as far as in me is. I will alfo ferve
" a Brother as much as lies in my Power, without being
" detrimental to myfelf or Family : and I will keep all my
" Brother's Secrets as my own, that fhall be delivered to
" me as fuch, Murder and Treafon excepted. All this I
" fwear, with a firm and fteady Refolution to perform the
" fame, without any Equivocation or Hefitation in me
" whatfoever, under no lefs Penalty than to have my Heart
" torn from my naked left Breaft, and given to the Vultures
" of the Air as a Prey. So help me God, and keep me ftedfaft
" in this my Fellow-Craft's Obligation. [*Kiffes the book.*]

Maf. Thank you, Brother.—After you received this Obligation, pray what was fhewn to you?

Anf. The Sign of a Fellow-Craft.

Maf. Pray give it me. *Anf.* I will, Right Worfhipful.

[He ftands up, and puts his Right Hand to his Left Breaft, keeping his Thumb fquare ; and his Left Hand raifed up, fo as to form a fquare.]

Maf. What was the next Thing done to you ?

Anf. He took me by the Right Hand, and gave me the Grip and Word of a Fellow-Craft, and the Pafs Grip†.

---

* A Cable Tow is three Miles in Length ; fo that if a Fellow-Craft is at that Diftance from his Lodge, he is not culpable on account of his Non-Attendance.

† The Pafs-Grip is thus performed : You muft put your Thumb-Nail between

(2⁷)

Maſ. What did they then to you ?

Anſ. He took me by the Right Hand, and ſaid Riſe, Brother *Bɔaz.*

Maſ. What followed after that, Brother ?

Anſ. He ordered me back, when every Thing I had been diveſted of was reſtored, and I was brought in again in order to return Thanks*.

Maſ. Being thus admitted, Brother, did you ever work as a Craft ?

Anſ. Yes, Right Worſhipful, in building the Temple.

Maſ. Where did you receive your wages ?

Anſ. In the Middle Chamber.

Maſ. When you came to the Door of the Middle Chamber, pray who did you ſee?   *Anſ.* A Warden.

Maſ. What did he demand of you ?

Anſ. The Paſs-word of a Fellow-Craft.

Maſ. Did you give it him ?   *Anſ.* I did, Right Worſhipful.

Maſ. Pray what is it ?   *Anſ.* SHIBBOLETH.

Maſ. How got you to the Middle Chamber ?

Anſ. Through the Porch.

Maſ. Did you ſee any Thing worth you Notice ?

Anſ. I did, Right Worſhipful.

Maſ. What was it ?   *Anſ.* Two fine Braſs Pillars.

Maſ. What are their Names ?

Anſ. JACHIN and BOAZ.

Maſ. How high were theſe Pillars ?

Anſ. Thirty-five Cubits, with a Chapiter Five Cubits †, which made it Forty in the whole.

[This is deſcribed more clearly in the Third Chapter of the Second Book of Chronicles, Verſe 15th.]

Maſ. What were they ornamented with, Brother ?

Anſ. Two Chapiters, each Five Cubits in Height.

Maſ. What were they adorned with beſides ?

Anſ. Lilly-work, Net-work, and Pomegranates.

Maſ. Were they hollow, Brother ?

Anſ. Yes, Right Worſhipful.

Maſ. How thick was the outſide Coat? *Anſ.* Four Inches.

Maſ. Where were they caſt ?

---

between the Firſt and Second Joint of the Right Hand, and whiſper the Word SHIBBOLETH. The Grip of a Fellow-Craft is by putting the Thumb-Nail on the Second Joint of the Right Hand, and the Word is BOAZ.

* The Ceremony of returning Thanks is the ſame as the Entered Apprentice's, excepting *for admitting me a Fellow-Craft.*

† The Reader is here to underſtand that there are three Sorts of Cubits ; the King's Cubit, three Engliſh Feet ; the Holy Cubit, one Foot ſix Inches ; and the common Cubit, twenty one Inches. The Cubit mentioned in the Old Teſtament is the Holy Cubit, which is one Foot ſix Inches.

Anſ.

(25)

Anf. On the Plain of *Jordan*, between *Succoth* and *Zartha*, in a Clay Ground, where all *Solomon*'s holy Veffels were caft.

Maf. Who caft them, Brother?

Anf. *Hiram Abiff*, the Widow's Son.

This generally finishes the Fellow-Craft's Lecture, and very few Lodges go fo far in their Queftions and Anfwers: Therefore, in order to enliven the Company, the Mafter afks fome good Singer to favour them with the following Song, which I have heard fung with great Energy and Rapture throughout the Lodge; every Brother bearing a Part in the Chorus.

The FELLOW-CRAFT's SONG.

HAIL, Mafonry! thou Craft divine!
　Glory of Earth, from Heaven reveal'd,
Which does with Jewels precious fhine,
　　From all but Mafon's eyes conceal'd.
Chorus. Thy praifes due who can rehearfe,
　　In nervous profe, or flowing Verfe?

As Men from Brutes diftinguifh'd are,
　A Mafon other Men excels,
For what's in Knowledge choice or rare,
　　But in his Breaft fecurely dwells.
Chorus. His filent Breaft and faithful Heart.
　　Preferve the Secrets of the Art.

From fcorching Heat and piercing Cold,
　From Beafts whofe roar the Foreft rends;
From the Affaults of Warriors bold,
　　The Mafon's Art Mankind defends.
Chorus. Be to this Art due Honour paid,
　　From which Mankind receives fuch Aid.

Enfigns of State that feed our Pride,
　Diftinctions troublefome and vain,
By Mafon's true are laid afide.
　　Art's free-born Sons fuch Toys difdain.
Chorus. Ennobled by the Name they bear,
　　Diftinguifh'd by the Badge* they wear.

Sweet Fellowfhip, from Envy free,
　Friendly Converfe of Brotherhood!
The Lodge's lafting Cement be,
　　Which has for Ages firmly ftood.
Chorus. A Lodge thus built for Ages paft,
　　Has lafted, and will ever laft.

---

* Here the whole Lodge ftrike their Right Hands all at once on their Aprons, keeping as regular Time as the Soldiers in *St. James's Park*, when they ftrike their Cartouch Boxes.

Then

(26)

Then in our Songs be Juſtice done,
To thoſe who have enrich'd the Art,
From *Jabal* down to *Aberdour**
And let each Brother bear a Part.
Chorus. Let noble Maſons Healths go round,
Their praiſe in lofty Lodge reſound.

In Company the Fellow-Craft takes the Pot or Glaſs, and draws it acroſs his left Breaſt, and touches it ; the Penalty being this, that he would ſooner have his Heart torn from his Left Breaſt, and given to the Fowls of the Air, than diſcover the Secrets of Maſonry. Sometimes this is done with the Right Hand only, as it is leſs taken Notice of by Strangers.

Having given the Entered Apprentice and Fellow-Craft's Part, I now proceed to the third and laſt Degree of Maſonry, which is termed *the Maſter's Part*, it being performed in the ſame Manner as the other two, *viz.* by Way of Queſtion and Anſwer, and is as follows :

Maſ. **B**ROTHER, where have you been ?
    Anſ. In the Weſt.
Maſ. And where are you going ?   *Anſ.* To the Eaſt.
Maſ. Why do you leave the Weſt, and go to the Eaſt ?
Anſ. Becauſe the Light of the Goſpel was firſt ſhewn in the Eaſt ?
Maſ. What are you going to do in the Eaſt ?
Anſ. To ſeek for a Lodge of Maſters.

* Lord *Aberdour* was formerly Grand Maſter ; at preſent Lord *Petre* fills that Station ; and they make uſe of his Name accordingly. For the Entertainment of our Readers, the Editor obtained a complete Liſt of all the Grand Maſters, ſince the Year 1722, viz.

Francis Scott, Earl of Dalkeith,	Edward Bligh, Earl of Darnley,
Charles Lenox, Duke of Richmond Lenox and Aubigny,	H. Brydges, Marq. of Caernarvon,
J. Hamilton, Lord Paiſley,	Rob. Raymond, Lord Raymond,
Wm. O'Brien, Earl of Inchiquin,	John Keith, Earl of Kintore,
Henry Hare, Lord Colraine,	J. Douglas, Earl of Morton,
James King, Lord Kingſton,	John Ward, Lord Ward,
Tho. Howard, Duke of Norfolk,	Tho. Lyon, Earl of Strathmore,
T. Coke, Lord Lovell,	James Cranſtoun, Lord Cranſtoun,
Ant. Brown, Ld. Viſc. Montacute,	Wm. Byron, Lord Byron,
James Lyon, Earl of Strathmore,	John Proby, Lord Caryſfort,
John Lindſey, Earl of Crauford,	James Brydges, E. of Caernarvon,
Thomas Thynne, Lord Viſcount Weymouth,	Sholto Ch. Douglas, Lord Aberdour,
John Campbell, Earl of Loudon,	W. Shirley, Lord Ferrers, and the preſent Lord Petre.

By the above noble Liſt of Grand Maſters, ſuch as no Age, Society, or Kingdom could ever boaſt to have ruled them, Maſonry has been fixed on the ſolid Baſis it now ſtands.

Maſ.

Maſ. Then you are a Maſter Maſon, I preſume?

Anſ. I am ſo taken and accepted among Maſters?

Maſ. Where was you made Maſter?

Anſ. In a Lodge of Maſters.

Maſ. How was you prepared to be made Maſter?

Anſ. My Shoes were taken off my Feet, my Arms and Breaſt were naked, and I was deprived of all Metal. In this Manner I was led to the Door of the Lodge*.

Maſ. How got you Admittance?

Anſ. By three diſtinct Knocks.

Maſ. What was then ſaid to you from within?

Anſ. Who comes there?

Maſ. Your Anſwer, Brother?

Anſ. One who hath lawfully and truly ſerved his Time as an Entered Apprentice and Fellow-Craft, and now begs to attain the laſt and moſt honourable Degree of Maſonry, by being admitted a Maſter.

Maſ. How do you expect to attain it?

Anſ. By the Benefit of a Paſs-Word.

Maſ. Can you give me that Word, Brother?

Anſ. I can and will, Right Worſhipful.

Maſ. Pray give it me then.   *Anſ.* TUBAL CAIN†.

Maſ. What was then ſaid to you?

Anſ. Enter TUBAL CAIN.

Maſ. How was you diſpoſed of?

Anſ. I was led round the Lodge.

Maſ. Where did you meet with the firſt Oppoſition?

Anſ. At the Back of the Maſter.

Maſ. What did he demand of you?

Anſ. The ſame as at the Door.

Maſ. How did he diſpoſe of you?

Anſ. He ordered me back to the Senior Warden, in the Weſt, to receive proper Inſtructions.

Maſ. What were thoſe Inſtructions, Brother?

Anſ. He inſtructed me as I ſtood in the Weſt, *Firſt*, To ſhew the Maſter in the Eaſt the due Guard or Sign of an Entered Apprentice, and take one Step upon the Firſt Step of the Right Angle of an Oblong Square, with my Left

---

* The Difference between the Manner of preparing the Perſon for the Degree of Maſter and the Entered Apprentice and Fellow-Craft, is this: That the Entered Apprentice's Left Arm and Left Breaſt is naked, with the Left Shoe off; and the Fellow-Craft's Right Breaſt is naked, with the Right Shoe off.

† TUBAL CAIN was the firſt Perſon who made uſe of Braſs, Iron, and other Metals, and is ſaid to be the Inventor of Muſic. His Deſcent was from the fifth Generation of *Cain*. In Scripture it is ſaid he became famous in working Metals, which *Hiram* afterwards greatly improved.

E   Foot

(28)

Foot forming a Square. *Secondly*, To make two Steps upon the fame Oblong Square, and to fhew the Sign of a Fellow-Craft. *Thirdly*, I was taught to take two Steps upon the fame Oblong Square, with both my Knees bent, and bare; my Body upright, my Right-Hand upon the Holy Bible, both Points of a Pair Compaffes being pointed to my Right and Left Breaft, where I took the folemn Oath or Obligation of a Mafter-Mafon.

Maf. Brother, can you remember the Obligation you fpeak of?

Anf. I'll do my endeavour, Right Worfhipful, with your Affiftance.

Maf. Pray ftand up, and begin.

Anf. " I *A. B.* of my own Free Will and Accord, and in
" the Prefence of Almighty God, and this Right Worfhipful
", Lodge, dedicated to Holy St. *John*, do hereby and hereon
" moft folemnly and fincerely fwear, that I will always hale,
" conceal, and never reveal, this Part of a Mafter Mafon to
" a Fellow-Craft, any more than that of a Fellow-Craft to
" an Apprentice, or any of them to the reft of the World,
" except in a true and lawful Lodge of Mafters, him or them
" whom I fhall find to be fuch, after a juft Trial and Exami-
" nation.——I furthermore do fwear, that I will attend all
" Summonfes fent to me from a Lodge of Mafters, if within
" the Length of a Cable-Tow.—I will alfo keep all my Bro-
" thers Secrets as my own, Treafon and Murder excepted,
" and that at my own Free Will.—I will not wrong a Bro-
" ther, or fee him wronged, but give him Notice of all Dan-
" ger, as far as in my power lies.—And I alfo fwear, that
" I will conform myfelf to all the Laws and Inftitutions of
" this Lodge.—All this I fwear, with a firm and fixed Refo-
" lution to perform the fame, under no lefs Penalty than to
" have my Body fevered in two; the one Part carried to the
" South, the other to the North; my Bowels burnt to Afhes,
" and the Afhes to be fcattered to the four Winds of the
" Heavens, that no further Remembrance of fuch a vile
" Wretch may exift among Men (and in particular Mafons.)
" So help me God, and keep me ftedfaft in this my Mafter's
" Obligation." [*Kiffes the Book.*]

Maf. Thank you, Brother.——Pray what was fhewn you after you had received this Obligation?

Anf. One of the Mafter's Signs.

[This Sign is given by drawing your Right-Hand acrofs your Belly, which is the Penalty of the Obligation. Then he gives the Mafter the Grip of an Apprentice, who fays, What's this? The Perfon anfwers, The Grip of an Entered Apprentice.]

Maf.

Maſ. Has it got a Name?
Anſ. It has, Right Worſhipful.
Maſ. Will you give it me?
Anſ. JACHIN.
Maſ. Will you be of or from?　　　*Anſ.* From.
Maſ. From what, Brother?
Anſ. From an Entered Apprentice to a Fellow-Craft.
Maſ. Paſs, Brother.
[He puts his Thumb between the firſt and ſecond Joint, which is the Paſs-Grip, and you pronounce the Word SHIBBOLETH.]
Maſ. What was done to you after that?
Anſ. He took me by the Grip of a Fellow-Craft, and ſaid, What's this?
Maſ. Your Anſwer, Brother?
Anſ. The Grip of a Fellow-Craft.
Maſ. Has it got a Name?　　　*Anſ.* It has.
Maſ. Will you give it me?　　　*Anſ.* BOAZ.
Maſ. What was then ſaid to you?
Anſ. Riſe up, Brother BOAZ.
Maſ. Brother, what followed?
Anſ. He told me I repreſented one of the greateſt men in the World, *viz.* our Grand Maſter *Hiram*, who was killed juſt at the finiſhing of the Temple; and the Manner of his Death is thus related:

" There were originally fifteen Fellow-Crafts, who perceiving the Temple almoſt finiſhed, and not having received the Maſter's Word, they grew impatient, and agreed to extort it from their Maſter *Hiram* the firſt Opportunity they could find of meeting him alone, that they might paſs for Maſters in other Countries, and receive the Wages or Profits of Maſters; but before they could accompliſh their Scheme, twelve of them recanted; the other three were obſtinate, and determined to have it by Force, if no other Way could be found: their Names were, *Jubela*, *Jubelo*, and *Jubelum*.

" It being always the Cuſtom of *Hiram*, at Twelve at Noon, as ſoon as the Men were called off to refreſh themſelves, to go into the *Sanctum Sanctorum*, or Holy of Holies, to pay his Devotion to the true and living God, the three Aſſaſſins above-mentioned placed themſelves at the Eaſt, Weſt, and South Doors of the Temple. At the North there was no Entrance, becauſe the Rays of the Sun never dart from that Point.

" *Hiram*, having finiſhed his Prayer to the Lord, came to the Eaſt Door, which he found guarded by *Jubela*, who demanded the Maſter's Grip in a reſolute Manner; he received for anſwer from *Hiram*, that it was not cuſtomary

E 2　　　　　　　　　　　　　　　to

(30)

to afk it in fuch a Strain ; that he himfelf did not receive it
fo ; adding, that he muft wait, and Time and Patience
would brir g it about.   He told him farther, that it was not
in his Power alone to reveal it, except in the Prefence of
Solomon King of *Ifrael*, and *Hiram* King of *Tyre*.   *Jubela*
being diffatisfied with this Anfwer, ftruck him acrofs the
Throat with a twenty-four Inch Gauge.   *Hiram* upon this
Ufage flew to the South Door of the Temple, where he was
met by *Jubela*, who afked him the Mafter's Grip and Word
in like Manner as *Jubela* had done before ; and on receiving
the fame Anfwer from his Mafter, he gave him a violent Blow
with a Square upon his Left Breaft, which made him reel.
Upon recovering his Strength, he ran to the Weft Door, the
only Way left him of efcaping ; and on being interrogated
by *Jubelum* to the fame Purport, who guarded that Paffage,
(to whom he replied as at firft) he received a terrible Fracture
upon his Head with a Gavel* or Setting Maul, which oc-
cafioned his Death.   After this they carried his Body out at
the Weft Door†, and hid it under fome Rubbifh till Twelve

* When you come to this Part of the Ceremony of making a Mafter, it
occafions fome Surprife ; the Junior Warden ftrikes you with a twenty-four
Inch Gauge acrofs your Throat ; the Senior Warden follows the Blow, by
ftriking you with a Square on the Left Breaft ; and almoft at the fame Inftant
the Mafter knocks you down with the Gavel. This is the Cuftom in moft
Lodges ; and it requires no fmall Share of Courage, for the Blows are frequently fo fevere that the poor Candidate falls backwards on the Floor ;
and the greater h's Terror at this Ufage, the more the Brethren are pleafed.
This Cuftom favours too much of Barbarity ; and many Inftances can be
produced of Perfons in this Situation, who have requefted on their Knees to
be fet at Liberty, and others who have made their Efcape as faft as poffible
out of the Lodge.   The *French* and Natives of *Swifferland* have a more
ftriking and folemn Way of reprefenting the Death of *Hiram*.   When a
Brother comes into the Lodge, in order to be raifed to the Degree of Mafter,
one of the Members lies flat on his Back, with his Face disfigured, and be-
fmeared with Blood, on the Spot where the Drawing on the Floor is made.
His natural Surprife and Confufion immediately appears, and one of the Brethren generally addreffes him to the Purport following : " Brother, be not
" frightened ; this is the unfortunate Remains of a Worthy Mafter, that
" would not deliver the Grip and Word to three Fellow-Crafts, who had
" no Right to it ; and from this Example we learn our Duty, viz. to die
" before we deliver the Mafter's Part of Mafonry to thofe who have no
" Claim thereto."   On kneeling to receive the Obligation, the fuppofed
dead Brother lies behind you, and during the Time of adminiftering the
Oath, and reading the Hiftory of his Death, he gets up, and you are laid
down in his Place.   This is the moft material Difference between the *French*
and *Englifh* Method of making a Mafter Mafon : and that it is more agreeable
to Humanity than giving a Man a violent Blow on the Forehead with a Gavel,
muft be obvious to every Reader.

† In this Point the Mafons themfelves differ : fome of them fay, he was
not carried out at the Weft Door, but buried on the Spot where he was
killed in this Manner : The three Affaffins took up Part of the Pavement,
made a Hole, and covered him over with Stones as foon as they had cram-
med him in ; after which they conveyed the Rubbifh out in their Aprons, to
prevent Sufpicion.

o'Clock

o'Clock the next Night, when they met by Agreement; and buried him on the Side of a Hill, in a Grave fix Feet perpendicular, dug due Eaft and Weft.

Maf. After you was thus knocked down, what was faid to you then ?

Anf. I was told I reprefented one of the greateft men in the World lying dead, *viz.* our Grand Mafter *Hiram.*

Maf. Thank you, Brother.—Pray go on.

Anf. As I lay on my Back, the Mafter informed me how *Hiram* was found; and by what means the three Ruffians were difcovered, as follows :

" Our Mafter *Hiram* not coming to view the Workmen as ufual, King *Solomon* caufed ftrict Search to be made ; but this proving ineffectual, he was fuppofed to be dead. The Twelve Fellow-Crafts who recanted, hearing the Report, their Confciences pricking them, went to *Solomon* with white Aprons and Gloves, Emblems of their Innocence, and informed him of every Thing relative to the Affair, as far as they knew, and offered their Affiftance in order to difcover the three other Fellow-Crafts who had abfconded. They feparated, and divided themfelves into four Parties; three Eaft, Weft, North, and South, in Queft of the Murderers. As one of the Twelve was travelling on the Sea-fide, near *Joppa*, being fatigued, he fat down to refrefh himfelf: but was foon alarmed by the following hideous Exclamations from the Cliff of a Rock : " Oh ! that my Throat had been cut " acrofs, my Tongue torn out by the Root, and buried in " the Sands of the Sea at Low-water Mark, a Cable'sLength " from the Shore, where the Tide ebbs and flows twice in " Twenty-four Hours, e'er I had confented to the Death of " our Grand Mafter *Hiram !*"—" Oh ! (fays another) that " my Heart had been torn from under my naked Left Breaft, " and given a Prey to the Vultures of the Air, rather than I " had been concerned in the Death of fo good a Mafter !" " But (fays a third) I ftruck him harder than you both ; " 'twas I that killed him. Oh ! that my Body had been fever- " ed in two, and fcattered to the South and North ; my Bow- " els burnt to Afhes in the South, and fcattered between the " four Winds of the Earth, ere I had been the caufe of the " Death of our good Mafter *Hiram !*" The Fellow-Craft hearing this, went in Queft of his two Affociates, and they entered the Cliff of the Rock, took and bound them faft, and brought them to King *Solomon*, before whom they voluntarily confeffed their Guilt, and begged to die. The Sentence pafled on them was the fame as they expreffed in their Lamentation in the Cliff; *Jubela*'s Throat was cut acrofs ; *Jubelo*'s Heart was torn from under his Left Breaft ; and *Jubelum*'s Body was fevered in two, and fcattered in the South and North.

" When

" When the Execution was over, King *Solomon* sent for the Twelve Crafts, and desired them to take the Body of *Hiram* up, in order that it might be interred in a solemn Manner in the *Sanctum Sanctorum*; he also told them, that if they could not find a Key-Word about him, it was lost; for there were only three in the World to whom it was known; and unless they were present it could not be delivered. *Hiram* being dead, it consequently was lost. However, as *Solomon* ordered, they went and cleared the Rubbish, and found their Master in a mangled Condition, having lain fifteen Days; upon which they lifted up their Hands above their Heads in Astonishment, and said, *O Lord, my God !* This being the first Word and Sign, King *Solomon* adopted it as the grand Sign of a Master Mason, and it is used at this Day in all the Lodges of Masters.

Maf. Brother, when *Hiram* was thus found dead, how was he raised ?

Anf. By the Five Points of Fellowship.

Maf. What are these five Points of Fellowship ?

Anf. He was taken by the Entered Apprentice's Grip, and the Skin slipped off. Then he was taken by the Fellow-Craft's Grip, which also slipped off; and lastly, by the Master's Grip*.

Maf. Brother, it appears you could not have been raised but by the Five Points of Fellowship. Pray explain them.

Anf. Hand in Hand signifies that I will always put forth my Hand to serve a Brother as far as in my Power lies.—— Foot to Foot, that I never will be afraid to go a Foot out of my Way to serve a Brother.———Knee to Knee, that when I pray, I should never forget my Brother's Welfare. Breast to Breast, to shew I will keep my Brother's Secrets as my own.—The Left Hand supporting the Back, that I will always support a Brother, as far as I can, without being detrimental to my own Family.

Maf. Thank you, Brother.—But pray, why was you deprived of all Metal ?

Anf. Because there was neither Axe, Hammer, nor Sound of any Metal Tool heard in the building the Temple of *Solomon*.

Maf. Why so, Brother ?

---

* The Master's Grip is thus performed: you take a Brother with the four Finger Nails of your Right Hand, and press close into the lower Part of the Wrist of his Right Hand with all your Strength; your Right Foot to his Right Foot, and his Right Knee to your Right Knee; the Right Breast to that of your Brother, and your Left Hand supporting his Back. In this Position you whisper in his Ear MAHABONE, or, as in the Modern Lodges, MAC BENACH, which is the Master's Word.

4   *Anf.*

(33)

Anf. Becaufe it fhould not be polluted.

Maf. How is it poffible, Brother, that fuch a large Build-ing fhould be carried on without the Ufe or Sound of fome Metal Tool?

Anf. It was prepared in the Foreft of *Lebanon*, and brought down upon proper Carriages, and fet up with wooden Mauls made on Purpofe for the Occafion.

Maf. Why were both your Shoes taken off from your Feet?

Anf. Becaufe the Place I ftood on, when I was made a Mafon, was Holy Ground.

Maf. What fupports our Lodge?   *Anf.* Three Pillars.

Maf. Pray what are their Names, Brother?

Anf. Wifdom, Strength, and Beauty.

Maf. What do they reprefent?

Anf. Three Grand Mafters; *Solomon* King of *Ifrael*; *Hiram*, King of *Tyre*; and *Hiram Abiff*, who was killed by the three Fellow-Crafts.

Maf. Were thefe three Grand Mafters concerned in the building of *Solomon*'s Temple?   *Anf.* They were.

Maf. What was their Bufinefs?

Anf. Solomon found Provifions and Money to pay the Work-men; *Hiram* King of *Tyre* provided Materials for the Build-ing; and *Hiram Abiff* performed or fuperintended the Work.

(End of the Mafter's Lecture.)

The Form obferved at the Inftalment of a Mafter, and the other Officers, on St. John's *Day.*

THEY ar being expired, a proper perfon is fixed on by the Members of every Lodge to prefide over and govern the Societies in the Capacity of Mafter. The Qualifications for this Office are, 1*ft*, That he muft be regularly and lawfully raifed; 2*dly*, He ought to be a Man of good Character, and irreproachable in his private Conduct: 3*dly*, He muft be well verfed in the Laws and Conftitutions of the Order, and ought to be temperate, cool, and quite perfect in going through the before-mentioned Lectures, as all the Queftions are put by him, and he is often obliged to affift the Brethren in making the proper Anfwers*; for every Mafon fitting round the Table anfwers in his Turn, in the fame Manner as Boys at Church faying the Catechifm. This is termed *Working*. For Inftance:

---

* I have been in a Lodge, where the Mafter was quite ignorant of the common Rules of Grammar; frequently making fuch egregious Blunders, that the Brethren could fcarce refrain from burfting into Laughter; and often embellifhing his Queftions with, " Brethren you have *let a body know as how* " you cannot be raifed but by the Five Points of Fellowfhip, &c. *tell us which* " *they be.*"

Suppofe

(34)

Suppose a Brother meets another, and asks him if he was at his Lodge last Night? He says, Yes. Well, replied the other, *Did you work?* that is, did you go through the several Questions and Answers in any of the Lectures?—If any Member cannot, or does not chuse *to work*, when the Question is put, and it comes to his Turn, he gets up, and clapping his Hand on his Breast, addresses himself to the Master, and begs to be excused; then the Left Hand Man answers in his Room

The Brethren having chose a proper Man for this Office, and he being approved of by the Grand Master, they proceed to the Installing him as follows: He kneels down in the South Part of the Lodge, and the late Master gives him the following Obligation before he resigns the Chair, which he repeats:

" I—*A. B.* of my own Free Will and Consent, in the Pre-
" sence of Almighty God, and this Right Worshipful Lodge,
" dedicated to St. *John*, do most solemnly and sincerely swear,
" that I will not deliver the Word and Grip belonging to the
" Chair whilst I am Master, or at any Time hereafter, except
" it be to a Master in the Chair, or a Past Master, him or them
" whom I shall find to be such, after a due Trial and Examina-
" tion.—I also swear, that I will act as Master of this Lodge
" till next St *John*'s Day, and fill the Chair every Lodge
" Night, if I am within the Length of my Cable-Tow.—I
" likewise further promise, that I will not wrong this Lodge,
" but act in every Respect for the good of Masonry, by be-
" having myself agreeable to the rest of my Brethren; and
" maintaining good Order and Regularity in this Lodge, as
" far as lies in my Power. All this I swear, with a firm and
" stedfast Resolution to perform the same, under no less than
" the four following Penalties: My Throat cut across, my
" Tongue torn out, my Heart torn from my Left Breast, and
" my Body severed in two. So help me God, and assist me in
" this my Obligation belonging to the Chair."[*Kisses the Book.*]

The Past Master raises him up, and takes off the Jewels and Ribbon from his own Neck, and puts it on the New Master, taking him at the same Time by the Master's Grip, and whispering in his Ear the Word CHIBBELUM*; after which he slips his Hand from the Master's Grip to the Elbow, and presses his Nails in, as is done in the Grip of the Master under the Wrist.

---

* CHIBBELUM signifies a worthy Mason. The Origin of the Words and Signs among Free Masons was on this Account: *Hiram* the Chief Artichitect of the Temple, had so great a Number of Workmen to pay, that he could not possibly know them all; he therefore gave each Degree or Class, a particular Sign and Word, by which he could distinguish them more readily, in order to pay them their different Salaries.

The

131

(35)

The Senior and Junior Warden, Secretary, &c. receive the Obligation as the Master, except the Grip and Word; there being none peculiar to them.

Having now gone through the several Degrees and Lectures belonging to the Entered Apprentice, Fellow-Craft, Master, and the Manner of Instalment, I shall close the Work with a few general Directions, dividing them under the following Heads :

I. *A Description of the Ornaments worn by the different Officers when assembled in the Lodge, and their proper Places of sitting.*

The MASTER, who sits in the East of the Lodge, has the Rule and Compass, and Square hanging to a Ribbon round his Neck, and a Black Rod in his Hand, when he opens the Lodge, near Seven Feet high.

The SENIOR WARDEN, sits in the West, with a Level hanging by a Ribbon round his Neck, and a Column placed on the Table, about twenty-nine Inches long.

The JUNIOR WARDEN's Place is in the South, with the Plumb Rule hanging by a Ribbon from his Neck, and a C.... his Hand.

The SECRETARY wears the Cross-Pens, hanging in the same Manner.

The Senior and Junior DEACONS have each a Black Rod, with the Compass hanging round their Necks; the Senior sits at the Back of the Master, or at his Right Hand; the Junior at the Senior Warden's Right Hand.

The PAST-MASTER has the Compasses and Sun, with a Line of Cords about his Neck.

The TREASURER has a Key hanging from his Neck.

II. *The Manner of giving the Signs of each Degree, and the Word belonging to it, with the Fellow-Craft and Master's Clap.*

The Master's Sign, Grip, and Word, &c.

The Sign. I... the Right Hand edgeways across your Belly, which ... Penalty of the Obligation.

The Grip. Take hold of the Right Hand of your Brother with your Right Hand, and press the four Finger Nails hard under the Wrist of his Right Hand; put your Right Foot to his Right Foot; your Right Knee to his Right Knee; and his Right Breast to yours, with your Left Hand supporting his Back.

The Word is MAHABONE ; or, in some Lodges, MAC-BENACH.

The Pass Word is TUBAL-CAIN.

F

The

(36)

The Master's Clap, is by holding both your Hands above your Head, and striking them down at once upon your Apron, both Feet keeping Time. They assign two Reasons for this Sign, *viz.* When the twelve Fellow-Crafts saw their Master lie dead, they lifted up their Hands in Surprize, and said, *O Lord our God!* and that when *Solomon* dedicated the Temple to the Lord, he stood up, and lifting up both his Hands, exclaimed, *O Lord my God, great art thou above all Gods.*

The Fellow-Craft's Sign, Grip, Word, and Clap.

Sign. Put your Right Hand to your Left Breast, keeping your Thumb square, and your Left Hand upright, forming a Square.

The Pass-Grip, is by putting the Thumb Nail of your Right Hand between the First and Second Joint of a Brother's Right Hand.

The Pass-Word is SHIB. :TH.

The Grip is the same as the Pass-Grip, except pressing your Thumb Nail on the *second* Joint, instead of between the first and second.

The Word is BOAZ.

The Fellow-Craft's Clap is by forming the Sign of a Craft as above, holding your Left Hand square and upright; then clap your Right and Left Hands together; and afterwards strike your Left Breast with your Right Hand, and from thence give a Slap on your Apron, your Right Foot going at the same Time.

The Entered Apprentice's Sign, Grip, and Word.

The Sign. Draw your Hand across your Throat edgeways. The Penalty of the Obligation being this, that an Apprentice would sooner have his Throat cut than discover the Secrets of Masonry.

The Grip. Take a Brother with your Right Hand, and press hard with your Thumb Nail upon the First Joint of the Fore-Finger of his Right Hand.

The Word. Whisper in his Ear JACHIN.

The Master kneels upon both Knees in the Ceremony of Making.

The Craft kneels with the Right Knee.

The Apprentice with the Left Knee.

III. The Form observed in Drinking.

The Table being plentifully stored with Wine and Punch, &c. every Man has a Glass set before him, and fills

2   it

(37)

it with what he choofes, and as often as he pleafes. But he muft drink his Glafs in Turn, or at leaft keep the Motion with the Reft. When therefore a public Health is given, the Mafter fills firft, and defires the Brethren to charge their Glaffes; and when this is fuppofed to be done, the Mafter fays, *Brethren, are you all charged?* The Senior and Junior Wardens anfwer, *We are all charged in the South and Weft.* Then they all ftand up, and obferving the Mafter's Motion, (like the Soldier his Right Hand Man) drink their Glaffes off; and if the Mafter propofes the Health or Toaft with *three Times Three Claps*, they throw the Glaffes with the Right Hand at full Length, bringing them acrofs their Throats three Times, and making three Motions to put them down on the Table; at the third they are fet down, (though perhaps fifty in Number) as if it was but one: then raifing their Hands Breaft high, they clap nine Times againft the Right, divided into three Divifions, which is termed *Drinking with three Times three*, and at the End they give a Huzza.

Having at length gone through my Plan, I have nothing further to add than this, that the following is the beft Method for a Stranger to gain Admittance, being what I have often tried in many Places, in order to be fully fatisfied.

As foon as you come to the Door of the Lodge, you will find the Tyler on the Outfide, with a drawn Sword in his Hand, and a white Apron on. Afk him if there is a full Lodge? And tell him you fhould be glad of Admittance as a vifiting Member; taking care to provide yourfelf with a white Leather Apron, which you may fhew him as if by Accident. He will, perhaps, afk you what Degree you are of, and defire a Sign, which you may fhew him with Readinefs, and likewife inform him what Lodge you belong to.

It being contrary to the Rules of the Society that the Tyler fhould admit a Stranger, he will go in, and acquaint the Mafter, that fuch a Perfon (mentioning your Name, and the Lodge you told him you belonged to) craves Admittance. Upon which one of the Wardens will come out to examine you, Draw your Right Hand acrofs your Throat edgeways, and he will fay, " What's that?" Your Anfwer muft be " The due Guard of an Apprentice." Then he will take you by the firft Joint of the Thumb of your Right Hand, and prefs it hard with the Thumb-Nail of the Right Hand, and afk, " What's this?"—You muft immediately anfwer, " The Grip of an Entered Apprentice."—If he is not fully fatisfied with this, he will go further on in this Manner.

Quef. Has it got a Name?—You muft anfwer, " It has." Then he will afk you to give it him.

Anf.

(38)

Anf. I'll halve it with you.—Begin, says he.—*Anf.* JA.
Mafon. CHIN. *Anf.* JACHIN.

Quef. Will you be of or from ?   *Anf.* From.

Quef. From what? *Anf.* From an Entered Apprentice to
a Fellow-Craft. He will then shift his Thumb from the
Apprentice's Grip towards the Fellow-Craft's, and afk,
What's this ? *Anf.* The Pafs-Word of a Fellow-Craft.
Give it me, fays he. Whifper in his Ear SHIBBOLETH.
On this he will put his Thumb to the fecond Joint, and fay,
What's this ? *Anf.* The Grip of a Fellow-Craft. Has it
a Name? fays he. *Anf.* It has—Pray give it me. *Anf.* I
will letter it, or halve it with you. *Mafon.* I'll letter it
with you.—*Anf.* Begin. *Mafon.* No, you begin. *Anf.* B.
Mafon. O. *Anf.* A. *Mafon.* Z. *Anf.* BOAZ.

What I have here offered being more than fufficient, you
will be admitted, and you muft put your Apron on, and
take your Seat. If there fhould be a making that Night,
you will be perfect in the firft Principles, and know more than
one in ten who have been Mafons many Years, and have never
read this Book.

If you fhould, after this, chufe to go to a Lodge of Mafters,
the Ceremony is the fame as above; but you are interrogated
as to the Grip, Pafs-Grip, and Word of a Mafter, which
you cannot fail of anfwering by reading the Mafter's Part
before mentioned. In all this you muft take care not to betray any Fear, but put on an Air of Affu̶   ̶ce.

*The Ceremony obferved at the Free-Mafons Funerals, according
to ancient Cuftom.*

No Mafon can be interred with the Formalities of the
Order, unlefs by his own efpecial Requeft, communicated
to the Mafter of the Lodge of which he died a Member: nor
unlefs he had been advanced to the third Degree of Mafonry.

The Mafter of the Lodge, on receiving intelligence of his
Death, and being made acquainted with the Day and Hour
appointed for his Funeral, is to iffue his Commands for fum-
moning the Lodge ; and immediately to make Application, by
the Grand Secretary, to the Deputy Grand Mafter, for a legal
Power and Authority to attend the Proceffion, with his Officers
and fuch Brethren as he may approve of, properly clothed.

The Difpenfation being obtained, the Mafter may invite
as many Lodges as he thinks proper, and the Members of the
faid Lodges may accompany their Officers in Form ; but the
whole Ceremony muft be under the Direction of the Mafter
of the Lodge to which the Deceafed belonged; and he, and
his Officers, muft be duly honoured and chearfully obeyed on
the Occafion.

All

All the Brethren, who walk in Proceſſion, ſhould obſerve, as much as poſſible, an uniformity in their Dreſs. Decent Mourning, with white Stockings, Gloves, and Aprons, is moſt ſuitable and becoming. No Perſon ought to be diſtinguiſhed with a Jewel, unleſs he is an Officer of one of the Lodges invited to attend in Form, and the Officers of ſuch Lodges ſhould be ornamented with White Saſhes and Hatbands; as alſo the Officers of the Lodge to whom the Diſpenſation is granted, who ſhould likewiſe be diſtinguiſhed with White Rods.

In the Proceſſion to the Place of Interment, the different Lodges rank according to their Seniority; the Junior ones preceding. Each Lodge forms one Diviſion, and the following Order is obſerved:

The Tyler with his Sword;
The Stewards, with White Rods;
The Brethren out of Office, two and two;
The Secretary, with a Roll?
The Treaſurer, with his Badge of Office;
Senior and Junior-Wardens, Hand in Hand;
The Paſt-Maſter,
The Maſter.
The Lodge to which the deceaſed Brother belonged, in the
following Order; all the Members having Flowers, or
Herbs in their Hands.
The Tyler;
The Stewards;
The Muſic [Drums muffled, and Trumpets covered;]
The Members of the Lodge;
The Secretary and Treaſurer;
The Senior and Junior Wardens;
The Paſt-Maſter.
The Bible and Book of Conſtitutions on a Cuſhion, covered
with black Cloth, carried by a Member of the Lodge:
The MASTER.
The Choriſters ſinging an Anthem.
The Clergyman;

Pall Bearers; | The BODY, with the Regalia placed thereon and two Swords croſſed. | Pall Bearers;

Chief Mourner;
Aſſiſtant Mourners;
Two Stewards;
A Tyler.

One

(40)

One or two Lodges march, before the Procession begins, to the Church-yard, to prevent Confusion, and make the neceſ-ſary Preparations. The Brethren are on no Account to deſert their Ranks, change their Places, but keep in their different Departments. When the Proceſſion arrives at the Gate of the Church-yard, the Lodge to which the deceaſed Brother belonged, and all the Reſt of the Brethren, muſt halt, till the Members of the different Lodges have formed a perfect Circle round the Grave, when an opening is made to receive them. They then march up to the Grave, and the Clergyman, and the Officers of the acting Lodge, taking their Station at the Head of the Grave; with the Choriſters on each Side, and the Mourners at the Foot, the Service is rehearſed, an Anthem ſung, and that particular Part of the Ceremony is concluded with the uſual Forms. In returning from the Funeral, the ſame Order of Proceſſion is to be obſerved.

This is the whole of Maſonry in all its Branches; and I defy any Maſon to prove the contrary, being ready to anſwer any Queſtion propoſed, which muſt be carefully ſealed up, and directed for R. S. to be left with my Publiſher, mentioning the Name and Reſidence of every Perſon deſiring any farther Information. And as to any anonymous Letters or Threatnings on Account of this Publication, they will be treated with Contempt, let them come from what Quarter they will. I alſo declare, that I will always attend and viſit at the Lodges mentioned in the Introduction, or any others as I have done for ſome years paſt.

ODES, ANTHEMS, and SONGS, ſung in the beſt LODGES.

O D E I.

HAIL to the CRAFT! at whoſe ſerene Command,
The gentle ARTS in glad Obedience ſtand:
Hail, ſacred MASONRY! of Source divine,
Unerring Sov'reign of th' unerring Line,
Whoſe Plumb of Truth, with never failing Sway,
Makes the join'd Parts of Symmetry obey:
Whoſe magic Stroke makes fell Confuſion ceaſe,
And to the finiſh'd ORDERS gives a Place:
Who rears vaſt Structures from the Womb of Earth,
And gives imperial Cities glorious Birth.

To Works of Art HER Merit not confin'd,
SHE regulates the Morals, ſquares the Mind;
Corrects with Care the Sallies of the Soul,
And points the Tide of Paſſions where to roll:
On Virtue's Tablet marks her moral Rule,
And forms her Lodge an univerſal School,
Where Nature's myſtic Laws unfolded ſtand,
And Senſe and Science join'd, go Hand in Hand.

O may

(41)

O may her focial Rules inftructive fpread,
'Till Truth erect HER long neglected Head!
'Till through deceitful Night fhe dart her Ray,
And beam full glorious in the Blaze of Day!
'Till Men by virtuous Maxims learn to move,
'Till all the peopled World HER Laws approve,
And Adam's Race are bound in Brother's Love.

ODE II.

WAKE the Lute and quiv'ring Strings,
 Myftic Truths Urania brings;
Friendly Vifitant, to thee
We owe the Depths of MASONRY:
Faireft of the Virgin Choir,
Warbling to the Golden Lyre,
Welcome here thy ART prevail:
Hail! divine Urania, hail!
Here in Friendfhip's facred Bower,
The downy wing'd and fmiling Hour,
Mirth invites, and focial Song,
Namelefs Myfteries among:
Crown the Bowl and fill the Glafs,
To every Virtue every Grace,
To the BROTHERHOOD refound
Health, and let it thrice go round.
 We reftore the Times of old,
The blooming glorious Age of Gold;
As the new Creation free,
Bleft with gay Euphrofyne!
We with god-like Science talk,
And with fair Aftræa walk;
Innocence adorn the Day,
Brighter than the fmiles of May.
Pour the rofy Wine again,
Wake a louder, louder Strain!
Rapid Zephyrs, as ye fly,
Waft our Voices to the Sky;
While we celebrate the NINE,
And the Wonders of the Trine,
While the ANGELS fing above,
As we below, of PEACE and LOVE.

ANTHEM I.

GRANT us kind Heav'n what we requeft,
 In Mafonry let us be bleft;
Direct us to that happy Place,
Where Friendfhip fmiles on every Face,

Where

(42)

Where Freedom and sweet Innocence
Enlarge the Mind and cheer the Sense.

Where scepter'd Reason from her Throne,
Surveys the LODGE, and makes us one ;
And Harmony's delightful Sway
For ever sheds ambrosial Day ;
    Where we blest Eden's Pleasure taste,
    Whilst balmy Joys are our Repast.

No prying Eye can view us here ;
No Fool or Knave disturb our Cheer ;
Our well-form'd Laws set Mankind free,
And give Relief to Misery.
    The Poor opprefs'd with Woe and Grief,
    Gain from our bounteous Hands Relief.

Our LODGE the social Virtues grace,
And Wisdom's Rules we fondly :ace ;
All Nature open to our view,
Points out the Paths we should pursue.
    Let us subsist in lasting Peace,
    And may our Happiness increase.

ANTHEM II.

BY Mason's Art th'aspiring Dome
On stately Columns shall arise,
All Climates have their native Home,
    Their god-like Actions reach the Skies.
Heroes and Kings revere their Name,
While Poets sing their lasting Fame.

Great, noble, gen'rous, good, and brave ;
    All Virtues they most justly claim ;
Their Deeds shall live beyond the Grave,
    And those unborn their Praise proclaim.
Time shall their glorious Acts enroll,
While Love and Friendship charm the Soul.

SONG I.

[*Tune*, Attic Fire.]
ARISE, and blow thy Trumpet, Fame ;
Free-Masonry aloud proclaim,
    To Realms and World's unknown ;
Tell them of mighty David's Son,
The ·ise the matchless Solomon,
    Priz'd far above his Throne.

The

(43)

The folemn Temple's cloud-cap't Towers,
Th' afpiring Domes are Works of ours,
   By us thofe Piles were rais'd :
Then bid Mankind with Songs advance,
And through th' ethereal vaft Expanfe,
   Let Mafonry be prais'd.

We help the Poor in time of Need,
The Naked clothe, the Hungry feed,
   'Tis our Foundation Stone :
We build upon the nobleft Plan ;   } Chorus.
For Friendfhip rivets Man to Man ;   } *Three Times.*
   And make us all as One.

Still louder, Fame, thy Trumpet blow ;
Let all the diftant Regions know
   Free Mafonry is this :
Almighty Wifdom gave it Birth,
And Heav'n has fix'd it here on Earth,
   A Type of future Blifs.

SONG II.

[*Tune,* Rule Britannia.]

WHEN Earth's Foundation firft was laid,
   By the Almighty Artift's Hand,
'Twas then our perfect, our perfect Laws were made,
   Eftablifh'd by his ftrict Command.
Cho. Hail, myfterious ; Hail, glorious Mafonry !
   That makes us ever great and free.

As Man throughout for Shelter fought,
   In Vain from Place to Place did roam,
Until from Heaven, from Heaven he was taught,
   To plan, to build, to fix his Home.
                Hail, myfterious, &c.

Hence illuftrious rofe our Art,
   And now in beauteous Piles appear ;
Which fhall to endlefs, to endlefs Time impart,
   How worthy and how great we are.
                Hail, myfterious, &c.

Nor we lefs fam'd, for ev'ry Tye,
   By which the human Thought is bound ;
Love, Truth, and Friendfhip, and Friendfhip focially,
   Join all our Hearts and Hands around.
                Hail, myfterious, &c.

G   Our

(44)

Our Actions still by Virtue blest,
  And to our Precepts ever true,
The World admiring, admiring shall request
  To learn, and our bright Paths pursue.
                              Hail, mysterious, &c.

SONG III.

[Tune, Goddess of Ease.]

GENIUS of Masonry descend,
  And with thee bring thy spotless Train ;
Constant our sacred Rites attend,
  While we adore thy peaceful Reign :
Bring with thee Virtue, brightest Maid,
  Bring Love, bring Truth, and Friendship here,
While social Mirth shall lend her Aid,
  To smooth the wrinkled Brow of Care.

Come, Charity, with Goodness crown'd,
  Encircled in thy heav'nly Robe,
Diffuse thy Blessings all around,
  To ev'ry Corner of the Globe ;
See where she comes with Power to bless,
  With open Hand and tender Heart,
Which wounded is at Man's Distress,
  And bleeds at ev'ry human Smart.

Envy may ev'ry Ill devise,
  And Falsehood be thy deadliest Foe,
Though Friendship still shall tow'ring rise,
  And sink thy Adversaries low ;
Thy well-built Pile shall long endure,
  Through rolling Years preserve its Prime,
Upon a Rock it stands secure,
  And braves the rude Assaults of Time.

Ye happy few, who here extend
  In perfect Lines from East to West,
With fervent Zeal the Lodge defend,
  And lock its Secrets in each Breast :
Since ye are met upon the Square,
  Bid Love and Friendship jointly reign,
& Peace and Harmony your Care,
  Nor break the adamantine Chain.

2   Behold

(45)

Behold the Planets how they move,
  Yet keep due Order as they run;
Then imitate the Stars above,
  And fhine refplendent as the Sun:
That future Mafons when they meet,
  May all our glorious Deeds rehearfe,
An' fay, their Fathers were fo great,
  That they adorn'd the Univerfe.

SONG IV.

[*Tune*, In Infancy, &c.]

L E T Mafonry from Pole to Pole
    Her facred Laws expand,
Far as the mighty Waters roll,
  To wafh remoteft Land:
That Virtue has not left Mankind,
  Her focial Maxims prove,
For ftamp'd upon the Mafon's Mind,
  Are Unity and Love.

Afcending to her native Sky,
  Let Mafonry increafe;
^ glorious Pillar rais'd on high,
  Integrity its Bafe.
  :e adds to Olive Boughs, entwin'd,
    An emblematic Dove,
As ftamp'd upon the Mafon's Mind
  Are Unity and Love.

SONG V.

L E T Drunkards boaft the Pow'r of Wine,
    And reel from Side to Side;
Let Lovers kneel at Beauty's Shrine,
  The Sport of Female Pride:
Be ours the more exalted Part,
To celebrate the Mafon's Art,
  And fpread its Praifes wide.

To Dens and Thickets dark and rude,
  For Shelter Beafts repair;
With Sticks and Straws the feather'd Brood,
  Sufpend their Nefts in Air:
And Man untaught, as wild as thefe,
Binds up fad Huts with Boughs of Trees,
  And feeds on wretched Fare.

G 2

But

(46)

But Science dawning in his Mind;
  The Quarry he explores;
Induftry and the Arts combin'd,
  Improv'd all Nature's Stores:
Thus Walls were built and Houfes rear'd,
No Storms nor Tempefts now are fear'd
  Within his well-fram'd Doors.

When ftately Palaces arife,
  When Columns grace the Hall,
When Tow'rs and Spires falute the Skies,
  We owe to Mafons all:
Nor Buildings only do they give,
But teach Men how within to live,
  And yield to Reafon's Call.

All Party Quarrels they deteft,
  For Virtue and the Arts,
Lodg'd in each true Mafon's Breaft,
  Unite and rule their Hearts:
By thefe, while Mafons fquare their Minds,
The State no better Subjects finds,
  None act more upright Parts.

When Bucks and Albions are forgot,
  Free-Mafons will remain;
Mufhrooms, each Day, fpring up and rot,
  While Oaks ftretch o'er the Plain:
Let others quarrel, rant, and roar:
Their noify Revels when no more,
  Still Mafonry fhall reign.
Our Leathern Aprons may compare
  With Garters red or blue;
Princes and Kings our Brothers are:
  May they our Rules purfue:
Then drink Succefs and Health to all
The Craft around this Earthly Ball,
  May Brethren ftill prove true.

SONG

143

(47)

SONG VI.

KATE AND NED.

ONE Night as Ned crept into Bed,
   Beyond his ufual Hour,
His loving Kate, his conftant Mate,
   Began to fcold and low'r.
You naughty Man where have you been,
   No longer I'll be flighted,
Nor thus at Home will mope and moan,
   While you'r abroad delighted?

I own, dear Kate, 'tis fomewhat late,
   But hear me out with Patience,
All Wives you know, are bound to fhew
   Their Hufbands due Obeifance;
In Truth, dear Kate, 'tis fome what late,
   But put a fmiling Face on,
For I, this Night, am made a bright,
   Free and accepted Mafon.

If this be fo, I pray now fhow
   Some certain Sign or Token,
For Mafons can erect a Plan,
   Or ftop a Breach that's open.
I have a Breach, a huge wide Breach,
   That gives me much Vexation,
This if you ftop, you will o'ertop
   All Mafon's in the Nation.

Then Ned arofe, pull'd off his Clothes,
   Drew out his Line and Level,
He pl 'd his Plum beneath her Bum,
   And brought it to a Bevil;
He took his Gauge, his Nine-Inch Gauge,
   And plac'd it with a floping,
He fix'd his Stones like Inigo Jones,
   And left no Crevice open.

Dear Ned, fays Kate, you've done a Feat,
   A Feat of mighty Wonder,
And as for me, you plainly fee,
   I fairly do knock under.
I'd pawn my Gown, my Robe and Coat,
   My Cardinal with Lace on,
If you each Night would be a bright,
   Free and accepted Mafon.

SONG

(48)

SONG VII.

[*Tune*,—God Save the King.]

LET Mafons Fame refound
    Through all the Nations round,
  From Pole to Pole :
See what Felicity,
Harmlefs Simplicity,
Like Electricity,
  Runs through the whole.

Such fweet Variety,
Ne'er had Society
  Ever before :
Faith, Hope, and Charity,
Love and Sincerity,
Without Temerity,
  Charm more and more.

When in the Lodge we're met,
And in due Order fet,
  Happy are we :
Our Works are glorious,
Deeds meritorious,
Never cenforious,
  But great and free.

When Folly's Sons arife,
Mafonry to defpife,
  Scorn all their Spite ;
Laugh at their Ignorance,
Pity their Want of Senfe,
Ne'er let them give Offence,
  Firmer unite.

Mafons have long been free,
And may they ever be
  Great as of Yore :
For many Ages paft,
Mafonry has ftood faft,
And may its Gᴸ ᵒs laft
  'Till Time'ᵴ . . more.

New

(49)

New ODE, *written by a Member of the* Alfred Lodge, *at Oxford, and set to Music by Dr.* Fisher, *and performed at the Dedication of* Free-Masons Hall.

Sung by Messrs. Vernon, Reinhold, Norris, &c.

STROPHE.
AIR. Norris.

WHAT solemn Sounds on holy Sinai rung,
 When heavenly Lyres, by Angel-fingers strung,
Accorded to immortal Lay,
That hymn'd Creation's natal Day!

RECITATIVE, *accompanied.* Vernon.

'Twas when the shouting Sons of Morn
 Bless'd the great omnific Word :———
 " Abash'd, hoarse jarring Atoms heard,
 " Forgot their pealing Strife,
 " And softly crouded into Life,"
When Order, Law, and Harmony were born.

CHORUS.

The mighty Master's Pencil warm
Trac'd out of each the shadowy Form,
And bade each fair Proportion grace
Smiling Nature's modest Face.

AIR. Vernon.

Heaven's rarest Gifts were seen to join,
To deck a finish'd Form divine,
 And fill the sov'reign Artist's Plan ;
Th' Almighty Image stamp'd the glorious Frame,
And seal'd him with the noblest Name,
 Archetype of Beauty, Man.

ANTISTROPHE.
SEMICHORUS and CHORUS.

Ye Spirits pure, that rous'd the tuneful Throng,
And rous'd to Rapture each triumphant Tongue ;
 Again with quick instinctive Fire,
 Each harmonious Lip inspire :
Again bid every vocal Throat
 Dissolve in tender votive Strain !

AIR. Vernon.

Now while yonder white rob'd Train
 Before the mystic Shrine,
 In lowly Adoration join,
Now sweep the living Lyre, and swell the melting Note.

RECITATIVE. Reinhold.

Yet ere the holy Rites begin
The conscious Shrine within,
 Bid your magic Song impart.

AIR.

(50)

AIR. REINHOLD.

How within the wasted Heart
 Shook by Passion's ruthless Power,
 Virtue trimm'd her faded Flower,
To opening Buds of fairest Fruit.
 * *How from majestic Nature's glowing Face*
 She caught each animating Grace,
 And planted there th' immortal Root.

EPODE.

RECITATIVE, *accompanied.* NORRIS.

Daughter of God's, fair Virtue, if to Thee,
 And thy bright Sister, Universal Love,
Soul of all Good, e'er flow'd the soothing Harmony
 Of pious Gratulation————from above;
To us, thy duteous Votaries, impart
 Presence divine!————

AIR. Mr. NORRIS.

 The Sons of antique Art.
In high mysterious Jubilee
 With Pæan loud, and solemn Rite,
 Thy holy Step invite,
 And court thy list'ning Ear,
 To drink the Cadence clear
That swells the choral Symphony.

CHORUS.

To thee, by Foot profane untrod,
Their votive Hands have rear'd the high Abode.

RECITATIVE. REINHOLD.

 Here shall your Impulse kind
 Inspire the tranced Mind!

AIR. REINHOLD.

And Lips of Truth shall sweetly tell
 What heavenly Deeds befit,
The Soul by Wisdom's Lessons smit:
What Praise he claims, who nobly spurns
 Gay Vanities of Life, and tinsel Joys,
For which unpurged Fancy burns.

CHORUS.

 What Pain he shuns who dares be wise
What Glory wins, who dares excel!

 * *The Lines in Italic were omitted in the Music.*

OFFICERS

(51)

OFFICERS of the GRAND LODGE of ENGLAND,
For the Year 1797.

HIS ROYAL HIGHNESS
GEORGE AUGUSTUS FREDERIC,
PRINCE OF WALES,

Electoral Prince of Brunfwick and Lunenburgh; Duke of Cornwall and Rothfay; Earl of Chefter and Carrick; Baron of Renfrew; Lord of the Ifles; Great Steward of Scotland; Captain General of the Honourable Artillery Company of London; and Knight of the moft noble order of the Garter,

GRAND MASTER.

The Right Hon. the EARL of MOIRA, BARON RAWDON, &c. &c. &c.

Acting Grand Mafter.

Sir PETER PARKER, Bart. *Deputy Grand Mafter.*
Lieut. Col. GEORGE PORTER. *Senior Grand Warden.*
RICHARD BRETTINGHAM, Efq. *Junior Grand Warden.*
JAMES HESELTINE, Efq. *Gr. Treafurer (and P. S. G. W.)*
Mr. WILLIAM WHITE, *Grand Secretary.*
Rev. A. H. ECCLES, *Grand Chaplain.*
THOMAS SANDBY, Efq. *Grand Architect.*
Rev. WILLIAM PETERS, *Grand Portrait Painter.*
Chev. BARTHOLOMEW RUSPINI, *Grand Sword-Bearer.*

N. B. *The Grand Secretary attends at Free-Mafons' Hall, on the Bufinefs of the Society, on Tuefday and Saturday Evenings.*

PROVINCIAL GRAND MASTERS.

America, North, H. Price, Efq. of Bofton.
Antigua, William Jarvis, Efq.
Armenia, Dionyfius Manaffe.
Auftrian Netherlands, the Marquis de Gages of Mons.
Bahama Iflands, James Bradford, Efq.
Barbadoes, Hon. William Bifhop.
Bengal, Babar, and Oriffa, Richard Comyns Birch, Efq.
Berkfhire, Arthur Stanhope, Efq.
Bermuda Iflands, William Popple, Efq.
Bombay, James Todd, Efq.
Buckinghamfh. Sir J. Throgmorton, Bart.
Cambridgfhire, Rt Hon. Lord Eardley.
Canada, Sir John Johnfon, Bart.
Carolina (S.) John Deas, Efq.
Chefhire Sir Robert Salufbury Cotton, Brt.
Coaft of Coromandel, in the Eaft Indies, John Chamier, Efq.
Cornwal, Sir John St. Aubyn, Bart.
Cumberland, H. Ellifon, Efq.
Creek, Cherokee, Chickefaw, & Chactaw, Nations, in N. America, William Auguftus Bowles, Efq.
Denmark, Norway, &c. Prince Charles, Landgrave of Heffe Caffel.
Derbyfhire, Sir J. Borlafe Warren, Bart.
Devon, Sir Ch. Warw. Bampfylde, Bt.
Durham, Wm Henry Lambton, Efq.
Effex, George Downing, Efq.
Francfort on Maine, Circles of Upper Rhine, Lower Rhine, and Franconia, John Charles Brocaner, Efq.
Georgia, Hon. Noble Jones.
Gibraltar, &c. His Royal Highnefs Prince Edward.
Grenada, &c. General Rob. Melvill.
Guernfey, Jerfey, &c. T. Dobree, Efq.
Hanover, Electorate of, and Britifh. Dominions in Germany, Prince Charles of Mecklinburg Strelitz.
Hamburgh, Bremen, and Part of Lower Saxony, Doctor J. Godfried von Exter.
Hampfhire, Col. Sherbone Stewart.
Jamaica, Sir Adam Williamfon, K. B.
Kent, Doctor William Perfect.
Lancafhire, John Allen, Efq.
Leicefter & Nottingham, Ld Rancliffe.
Lincolnfhire, Rev. William Peters.
Maryland, Henry Harford, Efq.
Montferrat, William Ryan, Efq.
Naples and Sicily, kingdoms of, Duc de Sandemetrio Pignatelli.
Norfolk and City of Norwich, Sir Ed. Aftley, Baronet.
Northumberland, John Errington, Efq.
H   Oxford-

(52)

Oxfordshire, Doctor J. M. Hayes.
Piedmont, in Italy, Count De Bernez.
Poland, Count Hulsen, Pal. of Mscislaw.
Radnor, Charles Marsh, Esq.
Russia, his Excellency John Yelaguine,
Senator, &c. to her Imperial Majesty
the Empress of Russia.
St. Croix, John Ryan, Esq.
Shropshire, Staffordshire, Flintshire,
Denbighshire, and Montgomery, Hon.
and Rev. Francis Henry Egerton.

Somersetshire, John Smith, Esq.
Surrey, James Meyrick, Esq.
Suffolk, William Middleton, Esq.
Sussex, General Samuel Hulse.
Sumatra, John Macdonald, Esq.
Wales, South, Thomas Wyndham, Esq.
Warwickshire, Thomas Thompson, Esq.
Westmoreland, G. G. Braithwaite, Esq.
Worcestershire, John Dent, Esq.
Yorkshire, Richard Slater Milnes, Esq.

Representative of the Grand Lodge of England in Germany, Colonel Augustus
Graefe, Governor to H. S. H. the Prince of Mecklenburg, at Darmstadt.

GRAND STEWARDS.

For 1796.

Brother Sir John Eamer, President.
L. R. Mackintosh, Treas.
James Duberly, Sec.
William Veel.
Joseph Dennison.
Robert Sutton.
Thomas Harper.
Thomas Caulfield.
William Greening.
John Hunter.
Thomas Parks.
William Bridgeman.

For 1797.

Brother R. H. Bradshaw.
Bailey Heath.
John Bullock.
Charles Turner.
Robert Harper.
T. A. Loxley.
Charles Millet.
John Pearth.
Joseph Heath.
John French, jun.
George Eves.
Samuel Roberts.

THE HALL-COMMITTEE

Consists of all past and present Grand Officers, and Mr. John Yeomans.

OFFICERS of the GRAND LODGE of ENGLAND, from its Revival, A. D. 1717, to the present Time.

GRAND MASTERS.

1717 Anthony Sayer, Esq.
1718 George Payne, Esq.
1719 J. T. Desaguliers, LL.D. F.R.S.
1720 George Payne, Esq.
1721 John, D. of Montague
1722 Philip, D. of Wharton
1723 Francis Scott, E. of Dalkeith
1724 Cha. Lenox, D. of Richmond
1725 James Hamilton, Lord Paisley
1726 Wm. O'Brien, E. of Inchiquin
1727 Henry Hare, Ld Coleraine
1728 James King, Ld Kingston
1729-30 T. Howard, D. of Norfolk
1731 T. Coke, Ld Lovel, afterwards
E. of Leicester.
1732 Ant. Brown, Ld Visc. Montague
1733 James Lyon, E. of Strathmore

1734 John Lindsey, E. of Crawford
1735 T. Thynne, Ld Visc. Weymouth
1736 John Campbell, E. of Laudon
1737 Edward Bligh, E. of Darnley
1738 H. Bridges, Marq. of Carnarvon
1739 Robert Ld Raymond
1740 John Keith, E. of Kintore
1741 James Douglas, E. of Morton
1742-3 John Ld Visc. Dudley and Ward
1744 Tho. Lyon, E. of Strathmore
1745-46 James Ld Cranstoun
1747-51 William Byron, Ld Byron
1752-53 John Proby, Ld Carysfort
1754-56 James Bridges, Marq. of Carnarvon, afterw. D. of Chandos
1757-61 Sholto Douglas, Ld Aberdour
1762-63 Washing. Shirley, E. Ferrers
1764-66

4

(53)

1764-66 Cadwalladar, Ld Blaney	1777-82 G. Montagus, D. of Manchester
1767-71 H. Somerset, D. of Beaufort	1783-90 His R. H. D. of Cumberland
1772-78 Robert Edward, Ld Petre	1791-96 His R. H. the Prince of Wales.

DEPUTY GRAND-MASTERS.

1721 John Beal, M. D.	1741 Martin Clare, A. M. F. R. S.
1722-23 J. Th. Defaguliers, LL.D. F. R. S.	1742-43 Sir Robert Lawley, Bart.
1724 Martin Folkes, Esq.	1744 William Vaughan, Esq.
1725 J. Th. Defaguliers, LL.D.	1745-46 Edw. Hody, M. D. F. R. S.
1726 William Cowper, Esq.	1747-51 Fotherley Baker, Esq.
1727 Alexander Choke, Esq.	1752-56 Tho. Manningham, M. D.
1728-30 Nath. Blackerby, Esq.	1757-61 John Revis, Esq.
1731-33 Thomas Batson, Esq.	1762-67 Col. John Salter
1734 Sir Cecil Wray, Bart.	1768-74 Hon. Charles Dillon
1735-38 Jh. Ward, Esq. after. Ld Ward	1775-86 Rowland Holt, Esq.
1739-40 W. Graeme, M. D. F. R. S.	1787-96 Sir Peter Parker. Bart.

GRAND WARDENS.

1717 Capt. John Elliot	1738 Lord George Graham
Jacobus Lamball	Capt. Andrew Robinson
1718 John Cordwell	1739 J. Harvey Thursby, Esq.
Thomas Morrice	Robert Foy, Esq.
1720 Thomas Hobby	1740 James Ruck, Esq.
Richard Ware	W. Vaughan, Esq.
1721 Josiah Villeneau	1741 W. Vaughan, Esq.
Thomas Morrice	Benjamin Gascoyne, Esq.
1722 Joshua Timson	1742-43 E. Ford, M. D. F. R. S.
J. Anderson, A. M.	S. Berrington, Esq.
1723 Francis Sorrel, Esq.	1744 W. Graeme, M. D. F. R. S.
John Senex	Fotherly Baker, Esq.
1714 George Payne, Esq.	1745-46 Fotherly Baker, Esq.
Francis Sorrel, Esq.	Thomas Smith, Esq.
1725 Col. D. Houghton	1747-51 Hon. Rob. Shirley
Sir Thomas Pendergast, Bart.	Thomas Jeffreys, Esq.
1726 Alexander Choke, Esq.	1752 Hon. J. Carmichael
W. Burdon, Esq.	Sir R. Wrottesley, Bart.
1727 Nathaniel Blackerby, Esq.	1753 Sir R. Wrottesley, Bart.
Joseph Highmore	Francis Blake Delaval, Esq.
1728 Sir J. Thornhill, Knt.	1754 Fleming Pingstan
Mart. O'Conner	Arthur Beardmore
1729-30 Col. George Carpenter	1755 Hon. H. Townsend
Thomas Batson, Esq.	James Dickson, Esq.
1731 George Douglas, M. D.	1756 James Nash, Esq.
James Chambers, Esq.	Bern. Joach. Boetefeur, Esq.
1732 George Rooke, Esq.	1757 William Chapman, Esq.
James Moor-Smith, Esq.	Alexander Valdevelde, Esq.
1733 James Moor-Smith, Esq.	1758-59 J. Dickson, Esq.
Hon. John Ward	Thomas Singleton, Esq.
1734 Hon. John Ward	1760-61 G. Schombart, Esq.
Sir Edward Mansell, Bart.	Charles Massey, Esq.
1735 Sir Edward Mansell, Bart.	1762 Col. John Salter
Mart. Clare, A. M. F. R. S.	Robert Groat, Esq.
1736-37 Sir Robert Lawley, Bart.	1763 Robert Groat, Esq.
W. Graeme, M. D. F. R. S.	Thomas Edmonds, Esq.

H 2

1764

150

(54)

1764 Hon. **Thomas Shirley**
Thomas Alleyne, Efq.
1765 Ricnard Ripley, Efq.
Capt. Charles Tuffnal
1766 Peter Edwards, Efq.
Horatio Riple·, Efq.
1767 Hon. Charles Dillon
Capt. A. Campbell
1768 Rowland Holt, Efq.
Henry Jaffray, Efq.
1769 Rowland Holt, Efq.
Charles Ta lor, Efq.
1770 Rowland Holt, Efq.
Sir W. Williams Wynne, Bt.
1771 Sir W. Williams Wynne, Bt.
Wiliam Hodgfon, Efq.
1772 Sir Peter Parker, Knt.
William Atkinfon, Efq.
1773 John Croft, Efq.
J. Ferdinando Gillio, Efq.
1774 } Hatch, Efq. *vice* L. Wentworth
Henry Dagge. Efq.
1775 Thomas Parker, Efq.
John Hull, Efq.
1776 Col. John Deaken
George Harrifon, Efq.
1777 Capt. . . H. Pafcal
John Allen, Efq.
1778 Henry Dagge, Efq.
Charles Marfh, Efq.
1779 Right Hon. Ld Vifc. Tamworth
George Heffe, Efq.
1780 John Peach Hungerford, Efq.
Theoph. Tompfon Tutt, Efq.

1781 Sir John St. Aubyn, Bart.
James Galloway, Efq.
1782 Sir Herbert Mackworth, Bart.
Philip Champ. Crefpigny, Efq.
1783 Hon. Wafhington Shirley
Geo. William Carrington, Efq.
1784 Hon. William Ward
James Meyrick, Efq.
1785 James Hefeltine, Efq.
M. J Levy, Efq.
Sir Lionel Darell, Bart.
1786 Sir Nicholas Nugent, Bart.
Nathaniel Newnham, Efq.
1787 Rt Hon. Ld Macdonald
James Curtis, Efq.
1788 Thomas Fitzherbert, Efq.
George Atkinfon, M. D.
1789 George Shum, Efq.
William Tyler, Efq.
1790 Henry Crathorne, Efq.
James Neild, Efq.
1791 Thomas Swanton, Efq.
John Warre, Efq.
1792 Thomas Thompfon, Efq.
Benjamin Lancafter, Efq.
1793 John Dent, Efq.
Edmund Armftrong, Efq.
1794 John Dawes, Efq.
Arthur Tegart, Efq.
1795 John Meyrick, Efq.
George Corry, Efq.
1796 George Porter, Efq.
Richard Brettingham, Efq.

GRAND TREASURERS.

1730-37 Nath. Blackerby, Efq.
1738-52 John Jeffe, Efq.
1753-65 George Clarke, Efq.

1766-85 Rowland Berkeley, Efq.
1786 96 James Hefeltine, Efq.

GRAND SECRETARIES.

1723-25 William Cowper, Efq.
1726 Edward Wilfon
1727-33 William head
1734-56 John Revis, Efq.
1757-67 Samuel Spencer

1768 Thomas French
1769-80 James Hefeltine, Efq.
1780-84 { James Hefeltine, Efq.
{ William White
1784 96 William White

GRAND SWORD-BEARERS.

1733-4 George Moody
1745 Thomas Slaughter
1746-55 Daniel Carne
1756-66 Mark Adfton
1767-68 Thomas Dyne
1769-71 William Smith
1772-75 John Deuvas

1776-77 Francis Johnfton
1778 85 James Bottomley
1786 87 John Paiba
1788-90 James Bottomley
1791 Benjamin Lancafter
1791-96 Chev. B. Rufpini

GRAND

(55)

GRAND STEWARDS.

[Those marked P were Presidents; T. Treasurers; and S. Secretaries of their respective Boards.——The present Officers of the Stewards Lodge are specified in Italicks, and the Members of it are marked thus, *.]

1721 Josiah Villeneau	John Brydges, Esq.	John Ross, Esq.
1723 Henry Prude	Wyrriot Ormond, Esq.	Cha. Champion
Giles Clutterbuck	Arthur Moore, Esq.	Richard Sawle
John Shepherd	Vinal Taverner, Esq.	James Pringle
Capt. Benj. Hodges	Claud Crespigny, Esq.	Francis Blythe
Edward Lambert	William Blunt, Esq.	1737 Sir Bouch. Wray, Bt.
Charles Kent	Col. John Pitt	Lew. Theobald, M.D.
1724 Capt. Sam. Tuffnell	Henry Tatam	Geo. Bothomly, Esq.
Giles Taylor	Thomas Griffith	Cha. Murray, Esq.
Capt. Nath. Smith	Solomon Mendez	Capt. John Lloyd
Rich. Crofts	1733 John Ward, Esq.	Capt. Cha. Scott.
Peter Paul Kemp	John Pollexfen, Esq.	Peter M'Cullock
North Stainer	H. Butler Pacy, Esq.	Tho. Jefferys
1725 John James Heidegger	John Read, Esq.	Peter Leige
1726-27 Edw. Lambert	Wm. Busby, Esq.	Tho. Boehm, Esq.
1728 John Revis, Esq.	Philip Barnes, Esq.	Benjamin Da Costa
Edwin Ward	J. Misaubin, M.D.	Nath. Adams
Samuel Stead	John Dwight	1738 Capt. An. Robinson
Theod. Cheriholm	Richard Baugh	Robert Foy, Esq.
William Benn	Thomas Shank	Ja. Colquhoun, Esq.
Gerard Hatley	James Cosens	Wm. Chapman, Esq.
William Wilson	Charles Robinson	Henry Higden, Esq.
William Tew	1734 Sir Ed. Mansell, Bt.	Harry Leigh, Esq.
William Hopkins	R. Rawlinson, LLD. FRS.	St. Beaumont, M.D.
Thomas Reason	C. Holzendorf, Esq.	Moses Mendez
Thomas Alford	Isaac Muere, Esq.	Geo. Monkman
H. Smart	Prescot Pepper, Esq.	Stephen Le Bas
1729-30 John Revis, Esq.	Christ. Nevile, Esq.	Christopher Taylor
Samuel Stead	Rich. Matthews, Esq.	Simon de Charmes
Edwin Ward	Fotherly Baker, Esq.	1739 Jn. Chichester, Esq.
William Wilson	Sam. Berrington, Esq.	Edward Masters
Thomas Reason	John Pitt, Esq.	Jos. Harris
William Tew	Wm. Verelst, Esq.	Rich. Robinson
———— Pread	H. Hutchinson, Esq.	Paul Hen. Robinson
———— Bardo. sen	1735 Sir R. Lawley, Bt.	Isaac Barret
———— Bardo. jun	W. Græme, M D. F.R.S.	Nath. Old[1]a
Charles Hoare	Mart. Clare, A.M.F.R.S.	Alex. Pollock
William Serjeant	J. Theobald, M. D.	Tho. Adamson
James Chambers, Esq.	M. Schomberg, M D.	Thomas Parry
1731 G. Douglas, M. D.	Cap. Ral. Fairwinter,	Geo. Armstrong
J. Chambers, Esq.	Ch. Fleetwood, Esq.	Sam. Lowman
Tho. Moore, Esq.	Tho. Beech, Esq.	1740 Esquire Cary
John Atwood, Esq.	Robert Wright	Mansel Bransby
Tho. Durant, Esq.	Thomas Slaughter	W. Vaughan, Esq.
George Page	James Nash	John Fabe.
John Haines	William Hogarth	John Saint
William Milward	1736 E. Hody, M.D. F.R.S.	John Soudon
Roger Lacy	I. Schomberg, jun. M.D.	James Bernard
Charles Trinquand	J. Ruck, jun. Esq.	David Dumouchel
John Calcot	John Gouland	Bryan Dawson
John King	Benjamin Gascoyne	William Ruck
1732 George Rook, Esq.	Walter Weldon	Mich. Comyrne
J. Moor Smyth, Esq.	John Jesse	George Mason

(56)

1741	Count. E. Fr. Taube	1752	Hon. J. Carmichael	1757	Humphrey Jackson
	Daniel Carne		Sir R. Wrottesly, Bt.		Richard Hill
	James Wallace		Ber. Joac. Boetefeur		Fred. Van Gehren
	John Gordon		Robert Marcellus		Paul B----thon
	Peter Hamet		George Steidell		Joh. Young
	George Caton		Stephen Yonge		Robert Lloyd
	William Salt		Richard Lane		Kenrick Peck
	William Arnold		Thomas Taylor		John Darby
	Lewis de Vaux		Charles Wade		Langford Millington
	Edward Rudge		John Jourdan		Thomas Clegg
	Richard Shergold		Jof. Brenice		John Wildsmith
	James Spranger		George Forbes		Adam Nuttall
1742-3	Edward Trevor	1753	Peter Leigh, Esq.	1758-9	Adam Nuttall
	Talbot Waterhouse		John Price		Abraham Hitt
	Ro. Bateman Wray		Tho. Apreece, Esq.		Jonathan Scott
	Ant. Benn		H. Cap. W. Montague		Frederick Kohed
	Stephen Rogers		F. Blake Delaval, Esq.		Ralph Bates, Esq.
	Peter Le Maistre		Cap. Edw Byre		John Rowley
	John Trail, A. M.		James Shrudder		Philip Scriven
	Henry Liel, Esq.		William Biset		George Rudd
	Edm. Brydges		Mark Adson		Capt. Chas Tuffnell
	William Vol		Henry Smith		Thomas Williams
	Thomas Pownal		Buelde Banson		Obadiah Wright
	Jof. Lycett		Rich. Savage, Esq.		James Wheeley
1744	John Coggs	1754	Arthur Beardmore		1760
	Tho. Clipperton		James Dickson	P.	William Smith
	Tho. Leddiard, Esq.		Samuel Markham	T.	Row. Berkeley, Esq.
	Charles Dubuy		Samuel Spencer	S.	John Burrell
	Luke Alder		George Dumar		William Potier
	Robert Mitchel		David Humphreys		Robert Harding
	H. & Rev. O. Dawnay		Martin Capron		John Friday
	Wm. Mountaine		Hon. Cap. Ch. Proby		George Restell
	Thomas Griffiths		William Singleton		William Barbar
	Tho. Smith, Esq.		John Atkinson		John Ast, Esq.
	John Torr		Godfrey Springal		John Ramfry
	Peter Gordon		Thomas Douglas		Thomas Smith
1745-6	Francis Jackman	1755	Hon. Ho. Townsend		Robert Jones
	George Pile, M. D.		Rev. John Entick		1762
	John Villeneau		Rev. Martin Despres		Col. John Salter
	Geo. Powlett, Esq.		James Shepheard		Robert Groat
	James Whitworth		James Gifford		Robert Laurie
	William Rogers		Albert Vandevelde		Henry Jaffray
	John Stone		Christian Heineken		Sir Rich. Glynn, Bt.
	James Bennet, Esq.		Caspar Schomhart		Stephen Day
	James Wilsford		Frederick Maurer		William Chapman
	Tho. Chaddocke		Thomas Singleton		Francis Bickerton
	Robert Cheeke		William Townsend		Thomas Dyne
	Fleming Pinkstan		Charles Pearce		------- Dun
1747-51	Mat. Creyghton	1756	Thomas Haward		John Benson
	John Feary		Charles Hoyle		Bryant Troughton
	Peter Clerke		Martin Klincke		1763
	Rob. Shirley, Esq.		William Andrews		Joseph Power
	Robert Young		Thomas Cobb		Thomas Alleyne
	William Rogers		James Pollard		Christian Poppe
	Jof. Lycett		Henry Gunter		Capt. Motler
	John Spranger		Th. Marriott Perkins		Richard Wright
T.	Meningham, M. D.		Mark Goodfiesh		Philip Cole
	Pheafant Hartley		Joseph Axtel		William Hodgson
	George Clarke		Gabriel Rifoliere		Tho. Edmonds, fen.
	Col. S. Berrington		Charles Maffey		Charles Churchman

(57)

George Carnaby
Richard Hestor
Hon. Tho. Harley
  1764
Thomas Treflove
John Nix
James Alleyne
Thomas Shirley, Efq
Edward Hoare
Wm Aſhburner   P.
Jonathan Miechle   T.
John Collock   S.
James Burgeſs
Thomas Edmonds
Thomas Woolfey
William Wray
  1765
Ant. Keck, Efq.
Richard Ripley, Efq.
Ant. Ten Broeke
John Forbes
Peter Edwards
Joshua Kitfon   P.
Chriſt. Cotterel   T.
John Nix   S.
Joseph Dixon
Rice Williams
Horatio Ripley, Efq
George Forbes
  1766
——— Pye, Bſq.
Wm. Cuthbertſon
Robert James
Pingit. Blackwood
Dr. St. John
William Collins   P.
Ant. Daveyer   T.
Peter Laimillier   S.
Richard Dickfon
Ant. Girardot, Efq.
Geo. Paterfon, Efq.
John Mitchie, Efq.
  1767
P.   Capt. Al. Campbell
T.   Lieu. Col. Twiſleton
S.   F. Twiſleton, Efq.
Charles Taylor, Efq.
Thomas Brooke
*James Hefeltine, Efq.   P.
Thomas French   T.
Hon. Charles Dillon   S.
Nathaniel Serjeant
H. V. Oudermeulen
Edw. Shepherd, Efq.
Samuel Way, Efq.
  1768
P.   Rowl. Holt, Efq.
T.   Major John Deaken
S.   John Derwas
Richard Rofe Drew

John Bowman
John Richardfon   P.
William Settree   T.
Jervie Critchley   S.
John Maddocks
Francis Johnfton
James Leichman
Peter Rainert
  1769
Col. Ch. Rainsford
* * * * * *
William Birch, Efq.
Eph. Godlieb Muller
John Allen, Efq.
William Paterfon   P.
Thomas Settree   T.
Edward Knightley   S.
Thomas Lecon
Peter Veftenburg
Capt. P. Hardwicke
John Anderfon
  1770
Sir W. W. Wynne, Bt.   P.
John Dobbins   T.
Stephen Freneau   S.
Hon. H. S. Conway
William Eden, Efq.
Peter Anf. Dellus   P.
J. Farmer   T.
Jofeph Binley   S.
John Wilfon
Henry Dagge, Efq.
George Hayter
J. W. Holwell, Efq.
  1771
Sir T. Tancred, Bt
W. Atkinfon, Efq.
George Gillio, Efq.
Sir John Blois, Bt.
Dominic Mead, Efq.
Henry Chittick, Efq   P.
Thomas Brown, Efq.   T.
Alex. Moultre, Efq.   S.
John Brockbank
Ja. Bottomley
James Harrifon
Thos. Williamfon
  1772
Sir P. Parker, Bt.
*J. Galloway, Efq.   P.
I. Ferd. Gillio, Efq.   T.
Theob. Burke, Efq.   S.
John Townfon, Efq.
Thomas Evance, Efq.   P.
Thomas Parker, Efq.   T.
John Shaw   S.
John Johnfon
Hon. Edm. Butler
John Bailey, Efq.
*Bart. Rufpini

  1773
John Croft, Efq.
James Nield, Efq.
John Hull, Efq.
Hon. Tho. Noel
Robert Sparrow, Efq.
William Harris, Efq.
Naph. Franks, Efq.
William Crozier
John Ainflie
John Hewitt
Lowen Hoad
Thomas Daw
  1774
F. Minſhull, Efq.
Richard Barker, Efq.
Peter Simond, Efq.
John Hatch, Efq.
Sir T. Fowke, Knt.
Robert Butler, Efq.
George Durant, Efq.
Thomas Martin
Richard Templar
*Alexander Dow, S.
James Miſt
Robert Brown Efq.
  1775
Capt. C. Frederick
T. Tomfon Tutt, Efq.
*William White
Capt. A. Murray
Capt. George Smith.
Thomas Lynch, Efq.
Walter Smith, Efq.
William Atkinfon
John Turner
Cuthbert Potts
Edmund Smith.
Alexander M'Kowl
  1776
Capt. M. H. Pafcal
Char. Marfh, Efq.
Geo. Harrifon, Efq.
Tho. Meggifon, Efq.
Rd. Troward, Efq.
Fr. Sey. Cosky, Efq.
Rd. Drake, Efq.
James Crosby
Edward Trelawney
*John Bain
John Ducket
Aaron Bateman
  1777
Ja. Worfley, Efq.
R. Franco, Efq.
*Rev. John Frith, SW.
George Heffe, Efq.
John Cooper
Dr. Ifaac Sequeira
Rich. Gamon, Efq.

Dr. Reynolds — S.
Row. Dawk. Mansell
Edward Halfhide
*Adam Dunford
John Milla
1778
P. Hon. Ld C. Montag
T. Benjamin Lyon, Esq.
S. G. W. Carrington, Esq.
T. H. Broadhead, Esq.
Rt. Biggin, Esq.
Geo. Lempriere, Esq.
Thomas Wright
Jonathan White
J. Richiardi
*J. Yeomans
William Omans
John Pilkington
1779
P. The Earl Ferrers
T. Joseph Newton, Esq.
S. James Pears.
Annesley Shee
T. B. Handasyd
Fred. Abel, Esq.
George Grieve, Esq.
John Hempsted
Joseph Newnham
Jac. Torban
Rowland Minns
Andrew O'Brien
1780
P. Francis Franco, Esq.
T. C. Vanderstop, Esq.
S. Ol. Crom. Vile
Percival Pott, Esq.
*Sherborne Stuart, Esq.
J. P. Hungerford, Esq.
James Johnston
*Joseph Smith
*William Fry
John Serjeant
John Mettenius
*Wm. Collins, jun. Esq.
1781
P. M. I. Levy, Esq.
T. *Peter Plank
S. *John Marshall
Henry Cotton
John Ratcliffe
PhilipCrespigny, Esq.
John Kupky
William Fleming
George Hartman
Frederick Bach
William Hough
*Sir John St. Aubyn, Bt.
1782
P. Sir H. Mackworth, Bt.
T. Thomas Preston, Esq.

*Edward Hill
Samuel Benge
George Barclay
*James Carr — P.
*Fleming French — T.
B. Lancaster, Esq. — S.
William Mayne
John Paiba
*Robert Pingston
*Benjamin Skutt, Sec.
1783
Hon. Wash. Shirley — P.
James Meyrick, Esq. — T.
William Faden — S.
William Tyler, Esq.
W. Mitch. Sale, Esq.
William Morse
Abr. Nunes
Thomas Settree, jun.
*James Rowley
*Simeon Pope
*Samuel Fulham
*William Miller
1784
Hon. Wm. Ward — P.
*Isaac Serra, Esq. — T.
John Tho. Cox, Esq. — S.
*Henry Crathorne, Esq.
Earnest Cramer
Redm. Simpson
*Stephen Clark, Tr.
Thomas Lambert
John Miller
James Fozard
John Harris, Esq.
Isaac Lindo
1785
*Sir N. Nugent, Bt. — P.
N. Newnham, Esq. — T.
*J. J. Pritchard — S.
Lionel Darell, Esq.
Arthur Onslow, Esq.
Capt. Christ. Parker — P.
*John Ungerland — T.
*James Massey — S.
*James Johnston
Dr. Steph. Freeman
Isaac Moron
*Thomas Patrick
1786
RtHon.LdMacdonald — P.
Robert Ingram, Esq. — T.
*William Earle — S.
*Col. Tho. Swanton
Richard Baldwin
*Wm. Fynmore, Esq. — P.
*John Pierce — T.
George Wright — S.
*R. Dennison
A. Garcia

*Thomas Hartley
*Thomas Pugh
1787
*Thomas Croft, Esq. — P.
*Col. W. D. Clephane — T.
S. W. Wadeson, Esq. — S.
James Curtis, Esq.
Dr. T. S. Dupula
John Lewis, Esq.
G. Errington, Esq.
*Alexander Dewar
*Robert Lambert
D. Aguilar
Geo. Blaklton
Benjamin Lloyd
1788
Tho. Fitzherbert, Esq. — P.
William Shard, Esq. — T.
T. Calender — S.
George Atkinson
DuncanCampbell, Esq.
Robert Richordon
James Howell
Charles Wren
*Thomas Barber
*William Daw, J.H.
*Ephraim Franco
*E. Jendun
1789
*George Shum, Esq. — P.
Edm. Armstrong, Esq. — T.
John Byng — S.
R. Baddeley
J. Raincock, Esq.
*Robert Griffin
Sam. VitaMontefiore
*William Virgoe
*James Steers, Esq.
Tho. Thompson, Esq.
M. Lascelles
*John Edwards
1790
John Warre, Esq. — P.
Thomas Ingram, Esq. — T.
*Samuel Plaisted — S.
R. Molesworth, Esq.
*John M'Donald
*R. W. Jennings, Esq.
*Nicholas Lambert
*Joseph Nourse, Esq.
*Francis Virgoe
John Read, Esq.
*J. I. Cossart
*James Robinson
1791
*John Dent, Esq. — P.
*James Sayer — T.
*W. C. Clarkson — S.
*R. Brettingham
*R. W. Bridgman, Esq.

(59)

*William Marſh	* R.L.*Fladgate, P.M.*	*W. Blackſtone, Eſq.
* James Whittle	Col. William Draper	1796
* Edward Fitch	* David Gwynne P.	*Sir John Eamer
* William Pitter	*Thomas King T.	*L. R. Mackintoſh
Count Duroure	1794 S.	* James Duberley
*S. Clanfield P.	* Hon. T. J. Twiſleton	*William Veel
*John Meyrick, Eſq. T.	* Nath. Goſtling, Eſq.	* Joſ. Denniſon
1792 S.	* Rd Woodward, Eſq.	*Robert Sutton
P. *Rich. Harborne, Eſ.	*The Earl of Pomfret	*Thomas Harper
T. *E. D. Batſon, Eſq.	* Sir W. J. James, Bt.	*Thomas Caulfield
S. * James Bliſs	*ThomasFellowes,Eſ.	*W. Greening
Geo. Fred. Parry, Eſ.	*RichardGriffiths, Eſ.	* John Hunter
Will.Hen. Pigou, Eſq.	* John Ruſh, Eſq.	*Thomas Parkes
* Fran. L. Morgan	*Cha. Carpenter, Eſq.	*W. Bridgeman
* David Bucklee	* John Johnſtone, Eſq.	
* Robert Salmon	* JoſephKnowles, Eſq.	*The following were preſent-
Thomas Hyde	*Robert Randoll, Eſq.	ed as G. S. for 1797.
* William Martin	1795	*R. H. Bradſhaw
* Robert Beſt P.	*S. S. Baxter, Eſq.	* Bailey Heath
* James Bradſhaw, Eſ. T.	*George Bolton, Eſq.	* John Bullock
1793 S.	*Thomas Hill, Eſq.	*Charles Turner
P. *G.*Corry, Eſq. P.V.M.*	*Arthur Gower, Eſq.	*Robert Harper
T. * Arthur Tegart, Eſq.	*William Ayres	*T. A. Losley
S. * John Dickinſon	* John Godwin	*Charles Millett
*Charles Clarke	*William Newton	John Peareth
* John Dawes, Eſq.	* John Steward	*Joſeph Heath
* John Whitfield	*George Porter, Eſq.	* John French, jun.
* William Tremain	* Mat. Wilſon, Eſq.	*George Eves
*Don. Macdonald	*William Gill, Eſq.	*Samuel Roberts

LIST of SUBSCRIBERS to the HALL-LOAN, agreeable to a
Reſolution of the GRAND LODGE, on 21ſt June, 1779.

H's R. H. the D. of Cumberland, P. G. M.	
Duke of Mancheſter, P. G. M.	Earl Ferrers, P. S. G. W.
Lord Petre, P. G. M.	Earl of Antrim
Earl of Effingham, P. A. G. M.	Earl Ferrers, P. S. G. W.
Sir Peter Parker, Bt. D. G. M.	G. William Carrington, Eſq.
Rowland Holt, Eſq. P. D. G. M.	James Meyrick, Eſq.
J. Heſeltine, Eſq. P. S. G. W. and G. T.	Sir Lionel Darell, Bart. P. J. G.
Thomas Sandby, Eſq. G. A.	Nath. Newnham, Eſq. Ws.
John Croft, Eſq.	James Nield, Eſq.
Thomas Parker, Eſq.	Benj. Lancaſter, Eſq.
Henry Dagge, Eſq.	Rowland Berkeley, Eſq. P. G. T.
Sir John St. Aubyn, Bt.	Mr. James Bottomley, P. G. S. B.
Sir Herbert Mackworth, Bt. P.S.G.	Henry Harford, Eſq.
Hon. William Ward Ws.	Chev. Bartholomew Ruſpini
M. I. Levy, Eſq.	Mr. William Rigge
Sir Nic. Nugent, Bart.	Mr. Peter Plank
Thomas Dunckerley, Eſq.	John Beardſworth, Eſq.
William Hodgſon, Eſq.	William Pickett, Eſq.
William Atkinſon, Eſq.	Mr. John Pilkington
John Hull, Eſq.	Mr. John Hodges
George Harriſon, Eſq.	Benjamin Lyon, Eſq.
John Allen, Eſq. P.J.G.	Mr. Joſeph Procter
Charles Marſh, Eſq. Ws.	Percival Pott, junior, Eſq.
George Heſſe, Eſq.	Mr. Edward Hill
T. Tompſon Tutt, Eſq.	John Philip Merckle, Eſq.
James Galloway, Eſq.	Francis Franco, Eſq.
P. Champion Creſpigny, Eſq.	Sir Stephen Luſhington, Bart.

I

Sir

156

(60)

Sir Barnard Turner, Knt,	**L O D G E S.**
William Shard, Esq.	
Mr. William Fry	The Grand Stewards' Lodge
John Harris, Esq.	2 Somerset-house L. Freemasons Tav.
James Barbut, Esq.	3 L. of Friendship, Thatched-h. Tav.
Jacob Appleby, Esq.	12 L. of Emulation, Paul's-head Tav.
Mr. Richard Cox	19 Castle-l. of Harmony, Dodt. Comm.
Mr. Jessintour Rosea	23 St. Alban's Lodge, Dover-street
Mr. Henry Strickland	29 Britannic Lodge, Pall-mall
Mr. Alexander M'Kowl	39 Royal Cumberland Lodge, Bath
Mr. Robert Cook	46 Fountain court, Strand
Mr. George Donadieu	86 Prince George, Plymouth
Mr. William Barker	95 L. of Love and Honour, Falmouth
Mr. John Piper	114 Rose & Crown, Crown-st. Westm.
Robert Ingram, Esq.	146 Shakespeare, Covent-garden
Robert Butler, Esq.	162 London Lodge, Ludgate-street
Redmond Simpson, Esq.	211 Caledonian Lodge, Gracechurch-st.
Christopher Parker, Esq.	216 Tuscan Lodge, Holborn
Isaac Serra, Esq.	218 Gothic L. Crown, Tufton-street
Thomas West, Esq.	238 George and Crown, Wakefield
The Rev. Edmund Gardener	294 L. of Virtue, White Lion, Bath
Cha. Phillott, Esq.	358 Lodge of Jehosaphat, Bristol
Wm. Street, Esq.	369 Lodge of Liberty and Sincerity,
Milbourn West, Esq.	Bridgewater
Dr. Tho. Sanders Dupuis	403 L. of Honour, Broad-way, Westm.
Thomas Hartley, Esq.	407 L. of Nine Muses, St. James's-str.
H, Spirling, Esq.	411 Gnoll Lodge, Neath
Sam. Tysson, Esq.	462 Royal Gloucester L. Bell. Glouc.
Hugh Dixon, Esq.	474 Harmonic Lodge, Hampton-court

REMARKABLE OCCURRENCES IN MASONRY.

ST. Alban formed the first Grand Lodge in Britain A. D. 287	Book of Constitutions first published — — 1723
King Athelstan granted a Charter to Free-masons — 926	Grand Secretary first established 1723
Prince Edwin formed a Grand Lodge at York — 926	Grand Treasurer appointed 1724
Edwin the IIId. revised the Constitutions — — 1358	A general Fund proposed for distressed Masons — 1724
Masons' Assemblies prohibited by Parliament — — 1425	Committee of Charity established 1725
Henry VI. initiated — 1450	Provincial Grand Masters first appointed — — 1726
Grand Masters of the Knights of Malta Patrons of Masonry 1500	Twelve Grand Stewards first appointed — — 1728
Inigo Jones constituted several Lodges — — 1607	Lord Kingston gave valuable Presents to the Grand Lodge 1729
Earl of St. Alban regulated the Lodges — — 1637	Duke of Norfolk, ditto 1731
St. Paul's begun by Freemasons 1657	The Emperor of Germany initiated 1735
William the IIId privately initiated 1690	Grand Stewards Lodge first established — — 1735
St. Paul's completed by Freemason. 1713	Frederic Prince of Wales initiated 1737
Grand Lodge revived, Anthony Sayer, Esq. G. M. — 1717	Anderson's Edition of the Constitution-Book published 1738
Several Noblemen initiated 1719	Grand Hall built at Antigua 1744
Valuable MSS burnt by scrupulous Brethren. — — 1720	Public Processions on Feast Days discontinued — 1747
Office of Deputy Grand Master revived — — 1720	Grand Certificates first issued 1755
	Fourteen Persons expelled for Irregularity — — 1757

Entick's

4

157

(61)

Entick's Edition of the Constitution
  Book published — 1758
Fifty Pounds distributed in Charity
  abroad — — 1760
Several Persons expelled for Irre-
  gularities — — 1762
His Royal Highness the Duke of
  Gloucester initiated — 1766
A new Edition of Constitutions or-
  dered — — 1767
Henry Frederic Duke of Cumber-
  land initiated — — 1767
One Hundred Pounds sent to Bar-
  badoes for Sufferers by Fire 1768
Registering-Regulations commenced
  28 October — 1768
Plan of a Hall for the Grand
  Lodge approved 1769
Elegant Hall built by the Free-
  masons at Barbadoes 1772
Hall-Committee appointed by the
  Grand Lodge — 1773
Alliance formed with the Grand
  Lodge of Germany — 1773
King of Prussia incorporated the
  Society in Prussia 1774
Ground purchased for a Hall in
  London — — 1774
First Stone of Freemason's Hall
  laid — — 1775
Five Thousand Pounds raised by a
  Tontine towards building ditto 1775
Office of Grand Chaplain revived 1775
Appendix to Books of Constitu-
  tions published — 1776
Freemasons Hall dedicated 1776
Office of Grand Architect estab-
  lished — — 1776

Freemasons Calendar published by
  Authority of the Grand Lodge 1777
Anniversary of Dedication ordered
  to be kept — 1777
Several Masons imprisoned at Na-
  ples — 1777
Fees of constituting Lodges and
  making Masons raised 1777
Several Princes of Germany form-
  ed a Lodge — 1777
His Royal Highness the Duke of
  Cumberland elected G. M. 1782
Noorthouck's Edition of the Book
  of Constitutions printed 1784
His Royal Highness the Prince of
  Wales initiated — 1787
His Royal Highness Prince Wil-
  liam Henry initiated 1787
His Royal Highness the Duke of
  York initiated 1787
Increased Registering-Regulation
  on Town Lodges commenced
  5 May — 1788
Freemasons' Tavern rebuilt 1788
Royal Cumberland Freemason
  School instituted 1788
His Royal Highness Prince Ed-
  ward initiated — 1790
His Royal Highness the Duke of
  Cumberland, G. M. died 1790
His Royal Highness the Prince of
  Wales elected G. M. 1790
His Royal Highness Prince Wil-
  liam of Gloucester initiated 1795
His Royal Highness Prince Ernest
  Augustus initiated — 1796

General Meetings of the Society in 1796.

Committee of Charity	—	—	—	Friday, February 3.
Quarterly Communication	—	—	—	Wednesday, Ditto 8.
Committee of Charity	—	—	—	Friday, April 7.
Quarterly Communication	—	—	—	Wednesday, Ditto 12.
Grand Feast	—	—	—	Wednesday, May 10.
Country Feast	—	—	—	Wednesday, July 5.
Committee of Charity	—	—	—	Friday, August 4.
Ditto	—	—	—	Friday, Nov. 17.
Quarterly Communication	—	—	—	Wednesday, Ditto 22.

LODGES *erased* for not conforming to the Laws of the Society,
or *discontinued* on being united to other Lodges, since the
Alteration of the Numbers in 1792.

1794.
49 Lodge of St. George de l'Observ-
  ance, Covent garden
90 Sea-Captains Lodge, Leadenhall-
  street

294 St. John's Lodge, Newmarket
327 St. Peter's Lodge, Mount-street,
  united to Lodge of Prudence,
  No. 69, now the Lodge of
  Prudence and Peter

I 2

380 Lodge

(62)

380 Loge d'Éga'ité, *united* to the ancient French Lodge, No. 110, now Loge d's Amis Réunis
399 At Futty-Ghur, Bengal
409 Royal Navy Lodge, Gosport
431 Pythagorean Lodge, Richmond, Surrey
467 Harodim Lodge, *united* to No. 1, the Lodge of Antiquity

1795.

107 St. Michael's, at Schwerin, in Mecklenburg

174 St. Nicolas's Lodge, Harwich
311 Helvetic - Union Lodge, Leaden-hall-ftreeet

1796.

207 Star Lodge, Chefter
336 Impregnable Lodge, Sandwich
350 Lodge of Rural Friendfhip, *united* to No. 330, Lodge of the Nine Mufes
393 St. Margaret's Lodge, Dartmouth-ftreet, Weftminfter

LIST of LODGES, with their Numbers, as altered by Order of the Grand Lodge, April 18, 1792.

The GRAND STEWARDS' LODGE, (*conftituted* 1735,) Freemafons' Tavern, 3d Wed. from Oct. to May. Public Nights, 3d Wed. in March and Dec.

Time immemorial.

1 Lodge of Antiquity, Freemafons' Tavern. Great Queen-ftr. (formerly the Goofe and Gridiron, St. Paul's Church-yard) 4th Wednefday in Winter
2 Somerfet-houfe Lodge, Freemafons' Tavern, 2d and 4th Mondays

1721

3 Lodge of Friendfhip, Thatched-houfe Tavern, St. James's-ftreet
4 British Lodge, Nag's Head, Carnaby-fquare, 1ft and 3d Tuef.
5 Weftminfter and Key-ftone Lodge, Horn Tav. Palace-yard, 1ft Mond.

1722.

6 Lodge of Fortitude, King's Arms Tavern, Old Compton-ftreet, 1ft and 3d Wed.
7 Lodge of St. Mary-le-bonne, Cavendifh-fquare Coffee-houfe, 3d M.
8 Ionic Lodge, King's Arms, Brook-ftr. Grofvenor fq. 3d Wed.
9 Dundee-arms Lodge, their private Room, Red-lion-ft. Wapping, 2d and 4th Th.

1723.

10 *Kentifh Lodge of Antiquity, Sun Tav. Chatham,* 1ft *and* 3d M.
11 *King's Arms, Wandfworth, Surrey*
12 *Lodge of Emulation,* Faul's-head Tav. Cateaton-ftr. 3d M.
13 *Fraternal Lodge, Greyhound Tav. Stockwell-ft. Greenwich,* 4th *Tu.*
14 Globe Lodge, White Hart Tav. Holborn, 1ft Th.
15 Jacob's Ladder, Bolt and Tun, Silver-ft. Fleet-ft.

1724.

16 *White Swan, St. Peter's, Norwich,* 1ft *Wed.*

17 Lodge *of Antiquity, Three Tuns, Portfmouth*
18 Caftle Lodge of Harmony, Horn, Doctors Com. 1ft and 3d M. Win. 1ft M. Sum.
19 *Lodge of Philanthropy, Black Lion, Stockton-upon-Tees, Durham,* 1ft *and* 3d *Frid.*

1725.

20 Lodge of Cordiality, Chancery Coffee-houfe, Southampton-buildings, Chancery-l. 4th M.
21 Old King's-arms Lodge, Freemafons' Tav. 1ft Th. from Oct. to May, inclufive

1727.

22 St. Alban's Lodge, Thomas's Tav. Dover-ft. Piccadilly, 1ft M.

1728.

23 Lodge of Attention, Freemafons' Tav. 2d and 4th Th.

1729.

24 St. John's Lodge, at Gibraltar, 1ft Tu.

1730.

25 Caftle Lodge, White Swan, Manfel-ft. Goodman's Fields, 1ft Th.
26 The Corner-ftone Lodge, Thatched-houfe Tav. St. James's-ft. 2d M.
27 Britannic Lodge, Star and Garter, Pall-mall
28 *Well-difpofed Lodge, at the Cock, Waltham Abbey,* 1ft *Sat.*
29 Lodge of Fortitude, Crown and Thiftle, Eaft Smithfield, 2d W.

1731.

30 Sociable Lodge, Horn Tav. Doctor's Commons, 4th M.
31 *Medina L. Vire, Weft Cowes, S.* 1ft & 3d *Th. W. Th. near full Moon*
32 King's Arms, Marybone-ft. Piccadilly, 2d and 4th Tu.
33 *Anchor and Hope, Bolton-le-Moor, Lancafhire, Th. on or after full Moon*
34 *Sarum Lodge, a private Room, George-court, High-ft. Salifbury,* 1ft *and* 3d *W.*

35 St.

159

35 *St. John's Lodge, Half-moon, Fore-st. Exeter, 2d and last F.*
1733.
36 *Royal Cumberland Lodge, Bear Inn, Bath, 1st and 3d F.*
37 *Lodge of Relief, Swan, Bury, Lancashire, next Th. to every full M.*
38 *St. Paul's Lodge, Shakespear Tav. Birmingham, 1st and 3d F.*
39 Royal Exchange, Boston in New England, 2d and 4th Sat.
40 Valenciennes, French Flanders, 2d and 4th Sat.
1734.
41 Strong Man, East Smithfield, late the Ship, at the Hermitage, 1st Th.
1735.
42 *Swan, Wolverhampton, 1st & 3d Tb.*
43 Union L. of Freedom and Ease, Surrey Tav. Surrey-st. Strand, 2d Tu.
44 *Lodge of Industry, Rose and Crown, Swalwell, Durham, 1st M. and 3d S.*
45 Solomon's Lodge, Charles-town, South Carolina, 1st and 3d Th.
46 Solomon's Lodge, No. 1, Savannah, in Georgia, 1st and 3d Th.
47 *Angel, Colchester, 2d and 4th Tu.*
1736.
8 *King's Head, Norwich, last Tb.*
50 Constitutional Lodge, Old Crown & Cushion, Lambeth-Marsh, 4th M.
51 *Howard Lodge of Brotherly Love, Crown, Arundel, Sussex, 1st and 3d M.*
1737.
52 Parham L. Parham, in Antigua
53 City Lodge, Ship Tav. Leadenhall-st. 2d and 4th Th.
54 Lodge of Felicity, Queen's Arms Tav. St. James's st. 2d W.
55 Vacation Lodge, Star and Garter, Paddington, 4th W.
56 *Lodge of Affability, Castle Inn, New Brentford, 1st and 3d W.*
1738.
57 Royal Naval L. private Room, near Red-lion-st. Wapping, 1st & 3d W.
58 *Royal Chester Lodge, Feathers Inn, Bridge-st. Chester*
59 Baker's Lodge, St. John's, Antigua
60 Lodge of Peace and Harmony, Swan Tav. Fish-street-hill, 4th Th.
61 *Union Cross, Halifax, Yorkshire, 2d and 4th W.*
62 The Great Lodge, St. John's, Antigua, 2d and 4th W.
63 *Lodge of Fortitude, White Horse, Hanging Ditch, Manchester, 2d M.*
1739.
64 Mother Lodge, at Kingston, Jamaica, No. 1, 1st and 3d Sat.
65 Mother Lodge, Scotch Arms, at St. Christopher's, Basseterre, 1st Th.

66 Lodge of Sincerity, Joiners and Feltmakers Arms, Joiner-st. Southwark, 4th W.
67 Lodge of Peace and Plenty, Redlion, Horsleydown Lane, 2d Th. Master's Lodge, 5th Th.
68 Grenadiers' Lodge, Kings Arms, Brook st. Grosvenor-sq. 2d W.
1740.
69 Lodge of Prudence and Peter, Bell, Upper Mount-st. 4th Th. Master's L. 5th Th.
70 Star in the East, at Calcutta, 1st Lodge of Bengal
71 St. Michael's Lodge, in Barbadoes
1742.
72 Lodge of Unity, Thistle and Crown, Suffolk-st. Haymarket, 1st Th.
73 Old Road, St. Christopher's
74 The Union, Franckfort, in Germany, 2d and 4th Th.
1743.
75 Prince George Lodge, George-town, Winyaw, South Carolina
1747.
76 Bear, Yarmouth, Norfolk
77 Lodge at St. Eustatius
1748.
78 Angel, Norwich, 3d Tu.
79 *Prince George Lodge, Plymouth, 1st and 3d*
80 Castle and Lion, St. Peter's Mancroft, Norwich, 2d M.
81 Second Lodge, Boston, N. England, Br. Coffee h. King-st. 3d W.
82 No. 1. Halifax, in Nova Scotia
1750.
83 Marblehead Lodge, in Massachusetts-lay, New England
84 St. Christopher's, at Sandy Point
85 Newhaven Lodge, in Connecticut, New England
1751.
86 Unicorn, St. Mary's, Norwich, 2d and 4th W.
87 *Lodge of Love and Honour, Royal Standard, Falmouth, 2d & last Tb.*
88 *Three Tuns, Great Yarmouth, Norfolk, last W.*
89 *L. of Freedom, Pope's Head, West-st. Gravesend, 1st and 3d Tb.*
1752.
91 St. John's Lodge, Bridge-town, Barbadoes, 4th M.
92 George Lodge, Rose and Crown, Downing-st. Westminster, 3d Tu.
93 The Stewards Lodge, at Freemasons' Hall, Madras, (revived 1786)
94 St. Peter's Lodge, Barbadoes, 1st and 3d S.
1753.
95 Old Cumberland Lodge, Red lion, Old

(64)

Old Cavendish-ft. Oxford ft. 2d Tu.

96 Foundation Lodge, Freemasons' Tav. Great Queen-ft. 2d W.

97 United Lodge of Prudence, Horſe Grenadier, near North Audley ſt. Oxford-ft. 1ſt Th.

98 Lily Tav. Guernſey

99 *Faithful Lodge, Vauxhall-Gardens, Norwich, 1ſt and 3d W.*

100 Evangeliſts' Lodge, at Montferratt

101 *Legs of Man, at Preſcot, Lanca-ſhire, W. next before the full Moon*

102 Royal Exchange, Norfolk, in Virginia, 1ſt Th.

1754.

103 *Druids' Lodge of Love and Libe-rality, London Inn, Redruth, Corn-wall, 1ſt and 3d Tu.*

104 Roſe and Crown, Crown-ſt. Weſt-minſter, 2d Tu.

105 *Caſtle and Lion, St. Peter's Man-croft, Norwich, 1ſt and 3d M.*

106 *Scientiſic Lodge, Eagle and Child, Cambridge, 2d M.*

108 *St. James's Lodge, Crown Inn, Uxbridge, Middleſex, Th. neareſt full Moon*

109 No. 2, at St. Fuſtatius

110 Loge des Amis Réunis, Lewis's Coffee-h. Air-ſt. Piccadilly, 3d M.

111 *Lodge of Unanimity, Bull's Head, Mancheſter, 1ſt and 3d Tu.*

1755.

112 In the 8th or King's own Regiment of Foot, 1ſt and 3d Tu.

113 Glouceſter Lodge, Roſe Tavern, Roſe alley, Biſhopſgate-ſt. 3d W.

114 Lodge at Wilmington, on Cape-Fear River, North Carolina

115 *Sea Captains' Lodge, Freemaſons' T. St. Tho. Build. Liverpool, every other Th.*

116 Union Lodge, Charles-town, South Carolina, 2d and 4th Th.

117 Lodge of Regularity, Thatched h. Tav. St. James's-ſt. 4th W.

118 Lodge of Freedom and Eaſe, Three Jolly Butchers, Old-ſtreet-road, 4th V.

119 Swan, at York-town, in Virginia, 1ſt and 3d W.

120 *Wounded Hart, Norwich, 2d and 4th Tu.*

121 *Phœnix Lodge, Sunderland, Dur-ham, 1ſt & 3d W. Gen. 1ſt W. Maſt.*

122 Grand Lodge Frederick, at Hanover

123 *Loyal Britiſh Lodge, Boot Tav. Eaſt-Gate-ſt. Cheſter, 1ſt M.*

1756.

124 St. David's Lodge, King's Arms Coffee-houſe, Brook-ſt. 4th F.

125 A Maſters' Lodge, at Charles-town, South Carolina, 2d & 4th Th.

126 Port-Royal Lodge, Carolina, every other Wed.

127 Lodge of St. George, Iſland St. au Croix, in the Weſt-Indies

128 Burlington Lodge, Coach and Horſes, Burlington-ft. 3d Th.

1757.

129 *Sea Captains' Lodge, King's Head, High-ſt. Sunderland, 2d & 4th Th.*

130 Providence Lodge, in Rhode Iſland

131 Shakeſpear, Covent-garden, 3d Th.

132 St. Mary's Lodge, St. Mary's Iſland, Jamaica

133 *Lodge of Friendſhip, White Horſe Tav. Norwich, 2d W.*

134 Lodge of Cordiality, Golden-croſs, Charing-croſs, 1ſt W.

135 St. John's Lodge, Anne-ſt. New York, No. 2, 2d and 4th W.

1758.

136 *King's Head, Coltiſhal, Norfolk, W. near and before full Moon*

137 *Lodge of Unity, King's Arms, Plymouth, 2d and 4th M. and 1ſt Tu. Maſt. I.*

138 *Beaufort Lodge, Corniſh-mount, on the Quay, Briſtol, 1ſt and 3d Tu.*

139 Lodge at Bombay, in the Eaſt-Ind.

1759.

140 *Marine Lodge of Fortitude, Half-moon, Pembroke-ſt. Plymouth-dock, 1ſt and 3d Tu.*

141 *The Sun, at Newton-Abbot, De-vonſhire, 2d Tu.*

1760.

142 London Lodge, London Coffee-h. Ludgate-hill, 1ſt and 3d Tu.

1761.

143 Lodge of Induſtry and Perſeverance, at Calcutta, 2d Lodge of Bengal

144 *Reſtoration Lodge, private Room, at Prieſt-gate, Darlington, laſt Sa.*

145 Union Lodge, at Crow-lane, in Bermuda, 1ſt W.

1762.

146 *St. George's Lodge, Globe Inn, Exeter, 2d and 4th Th.*

147 *Britiſh Union Lodge, Golden-lion, Ipſwich, Suffolk, 1ſt Tu.*

148 Royal Frederic, at Rotterdam

149 *Royal Lancaſhire Lodge, at the Hole in the Wall, Colne, in Lan-caſhire, 1ſt Th.*

150 St. Alban's Lodge, Shakeſpear Tavern, Birmingham, 1ſt & 3d Tu.

151 Merchants' Lodge,

152 St. Andrew's Lodge, } at Quebec

153 St. Patrick's Lodge,

154 St. Peter's Lodge at Montreal

155 Select Lodge,

156 In the 52d Regiment } at Quebec of Foot,

157 Royal

(6₅)

157 Royal Navy Lodge, Three-kings Inn, Deal, 1ſt M.
158 Lodge of Friendſhip, Crown, Lynn-Regis, Norfolk, 3d F.
159 Lodge of Inhabitants, at Gibraltar
160 Palladian Lodge, Bowling-Green, Hereford, 1ſt Tu.
161 Door to Eternity, at Heldeſham, in Germany

1763.
162 Union Lodge, White-lion, Notting-ham, 3d Tu.
163 St. Mark's Lodge, South Carolina
164 Lodge of Regularity, St. John's Hall, Black River, Muſquito Shore, 1ſt and 3d Tu.
165 Old Black Bull, at Richmond, in Yorkſhire, 1ſt M.
166 Marquis of Granby Lodge, private Room, Old Elvit, Durham, 1ſt Tu.
167 L. of Amity, St. George's Quay, Bay of Honduras, 1ſt and 3d Tu.
168 Thorn, at Burnley, in Lancaſhire, Sat. nearest full Moon
169 Union Lodge, Angel and Crown, Criſpin-ſt. Spitalfields, 3d Th.
170 Royal Mecklenburg Lodge, Green Dragon, Croydon, Surrey, 1ſt and 3d Tu.

1764.
171 Royal Lodge, Thatched-h. Tav. St. James's-ſt. 1ſt F.
172 La Sageſſe, St. Andrew, at the Grenadoes
173 White-lion, at Kendal, in Weſt-morland, 1ſt W.
175 White Hart, Ringwood, Hants
176 Lodge of Harmony, Red-lion, Fe-verſham, 2d and 4th W.
177 Salutation, Topſham, Devonſhire, 2d and 4th W.
178 Lodge of Conſtitutional Attach-ment, Mitre, Tooley-ſt. 1ſt. Th.
179 Philharmonic L. at the Red-lion Inn, Iſle of Ely, Cambridgeſh. 1ſt M.
180 Caledonian L. Guildhall Coffee-h. King-ſt. Cheapſide, 1ſt M.
181 Lodge of Perpetual Friendſhip, Lamb Inn, Bridgewater, Somer-ſet, 1ſt and 3d M.

1765.
182 Lodge of St. John Evan. Two Blue Poſts, Charlotte-ſt. Ruſſel-p. Rathbone-p. 2d W.
183 British Social Lodge, White Bear, Old ſtreet-ſq. 3d Tu.
184 Tuſcan Lodge, King's Head Tav. Holborn, 3d Th.
185 Operative Maſons, Cannon, Port-land-road, Marybone, 1ſt Tu. Maſt. L. 5th Tu.
186 Gothick Lodge, Foot-guards Sut-tling-h. Whitehall, 4th M.

187 Old Antelope Inn, Pool, in Dorſet-ſhire, 1ſt and 3d W.
188 Corinthian Lodge, Tiger, Wells-ſt. Oxford-ſt. 3d M.
189 Tontine, Sheffield, in Yorkſhire, 2d Frid.
190 At Alloſt, in Flanders
191 St. George's Lodge, at the Caſtle, Lewiſham, Kent, 1ſt M.
192 Black Horſe, Tombland, Norwich, laſt F.
193 K. Edwin Lodge, Angel, Bury St. Edmunds, M. on or preceding full Moon
194 St. Luke's Lodge, Don Saltero's Coffee-b. Chelſea, 1ſt Tu.
195 Lodge at Joppa, in Baltimore County, in Maryland
196 L. of Perfect Friendſhip, White Hart Inn and Tav. Bath, 2d & 4th Tu.
197 At St. Hilary, in Jerſey
198 Swan, at Warrington, in Lanca-ſhire, laſt M.
199 Lodge of Perfect Unanimity, at Madras, No. 1, Coaſt of Coro-mandel (revived 1786)
200 Lodge, No. 1, Bencoolen
201 Tortola & Beef Iſland, 1ſt & 3d W.

1766.
202 Lodge of Unanimity, Black Bull Inn, Wakefield, Yorkſhire
203 King's Arms Punch-houſe, Shad Thames, 1ſt M.
204 English Lodge, at Bourdeaux, (have met ſince the Year 1732)
205 Bedford Lodge, Freemaſons' Tav. Great Queen-ſt. 1ſt W.
206 Patriotic Lodge, Greyhound, Croydon, Surrey, Th. after every full Moon
208 St. Nicholas' Lodge, White Hart, Newcaſtle-upon-Tyne
209 Sion Lodge, private Room, North Shields, Northumberland, 2d Tu.
210 Lodge of True Friendſhip, Seven Stars, Bromley, Middleſex, 3d Tu.

1767.
211 Angel, Upper Ground, Chriſt-church, Southwark, 2d Tu.
212 Lodge of Integrity, Bull's Head Inn, Mancheſter, 1ſt M.
213 Union Lodge, Riſing Sun, Caſtle Ditch, Briſtol
214 At Grenoble, in France
215 Lodge of Morality, King's Head, Old Compton-ſt. Soho, 2d Th.
216 Three Lions, Marborough, in Heſſia
217 Lodge of Honour and Generoſity, King's Head Tav. Holborn, 1ſtTh.
218 Lodge of Union, Three Jolly Hat-ters, Bermondſey ſt. 3d W.
219 Royal York of Friendſhip, at Ber-lin, Middle Mark of Brandenburg
220 British

(66)

220 British Union, Rotterdam
221 St. John's Lodge, Flask Tavern, Hampstead, 1st Th.
222 Three Pillars, Rotterdam
223 Royal White Hart L. Halifax, North Carolina
224 Lodge of Amity, White Horse, Preston, Lancashire, 1st and 3d Th. Win. 1st Th. Sum.
225 Lodge of Amity, private Room, Canton, in China
226 All Souls Lodge, Tiverton, in Devonshire
227 L. Friendship, Angel, Illford, Essex, M. nearest full Moon, Mich. to Lady Day

1768.

228 Lodge of Concord, White-lion, High-st. Bloomsbury, 3d Tu.
229 Mona Lodge, King's Head, at Holyhead, Anglesea, N. Wales, every 3d F.
230 La Victoire, City of Rotterdam, in Holland
231 L. Sincerity. Gregorian's Arms, near Jamaica-row, Bermondsey, 2d Tu.
232 Caveat Lodge, Angel, Hammersmith, 1st Tu.
233 In the 14th Regiment of Foot
234 Constant Union, the City of Ghent, in Flanders
235 Godolphin Lodge, St. Mary's Island, Scilly
236 Manchester Lodge, Nott's Coffee-h. Butcher-row, Temple-bar, 1st W.
237 Lodge of Perfect Union, in his Sicilian Majesty's Reg. of Foot, Naples
238 L'Espérance, Thatched-h. Tav. St. James's-st. 1st M.
239 Qu. Charlotte's Lodge, Ashley's Punch-house, Ludgate-hill, 2d Th.

1769.

240 Sun Lodge, in the City of Flushing, in the Province of Zealand
241 Lodge of Hope, Crown, Stourbridge, Worcestershire
242 Lodge of Unity, K. Henry's Head, Red-lion-st. Whitechapel, 4th M.
243 Royal George L. at Newton Abbot
244 Beaufort Lodge, at Swansea
245 Well-chosen Lodge, at Naples
246 Lodge of Virtue, White-lion, Market-place, Bath, 1st & 3d M.
247 Inflexible Lodge, White Hart, Mitcham, Surrey. W. nearest full M.
248 Lodge of Hospitality, Bush Tav. Corn-st. Bristol, 2d and 4th W.
249 St. Peter's Lodge, King's Head, at Walworth, 3d M.
250 No. 1, ⎱
251 No. 2, ⎰ at Sweden
252 No. 3, ⎰

253 Golden Lion, at Neston, Cheshire, 1st F.
254 Lodge of Sincerity, Phœnix Inn, Fore-st. Plymouth Dock, 2d and 4th M.
255 Lodge of St. John, Fleece Tav. Manchester, last M.

1770.

256 L. of Perfect Harmony, at Mons, in the Austrian Netherlands
257 Lodge of Friendship, Bunch of Grapes, Limehouse-hole, 2d and 4th W.
258 Lodge of Prosperity, Globe Tav. St. Saviour's Ch. Yd. Southwark, 2d W.
259 St. Charles de la Concord, in the City of Brunswick
260 Lodge of Fortitude and Perseverance, Fox, Epsom, Th. nearest full M.
261 White Hart, Christ Church, Hants
262 Lodge of Concord, private Room, Barnard Castle, Durham, 1st Th.

1771.

263 Jerusalem Lodge, Crown-t. Clerkenwell-green, 1st and 3d W. Mast. L. 5th W.
264 Lodge of Industry, Ben Jonson's Head, Shoe-lane, 2d Th.
265 L. of Perfect Union, at Leghorn
266 Lodge of Sincere Brotherly Love, at ditto
267 Lodge of Perfect Union, St. Petersburgh
268 Lodge of Friendship, Prince George, Fore-st. Plymouth Dock, 1st and 3d W. I. F. Mast. L.
269 Junior Lodge, Kingston, No. 2, in Jamaica
270 Harmony Lodge, Kingston, No. 3, in ditto
271 St. James's Lodge, Montego-bay, No. 4, in ditto
272 Union Lodge, St. James's Parish, No. 5, in ditto
273 Lodge of Harmony, Bush, Carlisle, Cumberland, 2d W.

1772.

274 Rising Sun Lodge, at Fort Marlborough, in the East Indies
275 Lodge of Vigilance, Island of Grenada
276 Lodge of Discretion, ditto
277 Torbay Lodge, Crown and Anchor, at Paignton, in Devon
278 Union Lodge, at St. Eustatius, in the West Indies
279 Lodge of Candour, at Strasbourg
280 L. of Friendship, Shipwrights' Arms, Deptford-green, 2d Th.
281 Lodge at Speight's Town, in Barbadoes
282 Lodge of Concord, at Antigua

283 Lodge

283 Lodge of the Three Grand Principles, King's Head, Iflington, Fr. on or near full Moon

284 *Royal Edmund Lodge, at Bury St. Edmunds, W. preceding or on full Moon*

285 Union Lodge, at Venice

286 Lodge at Verona

287 Lodge of Liberty, Half Moon, Weft Smithfield, 1ft Th.

288 Lodge of Unanimity, at Calcutta, 3d Lodge of Bengal

1773.

289 Lodge at Detroit, in Canada

290 *Apollo Lodge, at the Merchants' Hall, York*

291 *Lodge of Jehofaphat, Rummer Tav. Briftol,* 1ft and 3d *W.*

292 Anchor and Hope, Calcutta, 6th Lodge of Bengal

293 Lodge of Humility with Fortitude, Calcutta, 5th Lodge of Bengal

295 *Lodge of Union, private Room, Hill Gate, Town of Gatefhead, Durham*

296 Williamfburg Lodge, at Williamfburg, Virginia

297 Botetourt Lodge, at Botetourt, Virginia

298 Lodge Frederick, at Caffol, in Germany

299 L. of Good Friends, at Roufleau, at Dominica

1774.

300 *Lodge of Liberty and Sincerity, Crown Inn, Bridgewater, Somerfet,* 2d and laft *Fr.*

301 *Lodge of Prudence, Boot & Shoe, Leigh, in Lancafhire, W. next full Moon*

302 Unity Lodge, No. 2, at Savannah, in Georgia, 1ft and 3d F.

303 Lodge of the Nine Mufes, No. 1, at Peterfburgh, in Ruffia

304 Lodge of the Mufe Urania, No. 2, in ditto

305 Lodge of Bellona, No. 3, in ditto

306 Lodge of Mars, No. 4, at Yafly, in ditto

307 Lodge of the Mufe Clio, No. 5, at Mofcow, in ditto

308 *St. Bede's Lodge, Spread Eagle, Morpeth, Northumberland,* 2d & 4th *M.*

309 Lodge of Harmony, at Guernfey

1775.

310 *Durnovarian Lodge, Royal Oak, Dorchefter, Dorfet*

312 *Sun and Sector, Workington, in Cumberland,* 1ft *M.*

313 St. Jean de Nouvelle Efpérance, in Turin

314 *True and Faithful Lodge, White Bear, Weft Malling, in Kent, laft M.*

315 Grenadiers' Lodge, at Savannah, in Georgia, 1ft and 3d G.

316 L. of True Friendfhip, with the 3d Brigade, 4th L. of Bengal

317 Green Ifland L. at Green Ifland, No. 8, in Jamaica

318 L. of Lucca, Parifh of Hanover, No. 9, in ditto

319 Union L. at Savannah la Mar, No. 11, in ditto

320 Union L. at Detroit, in Canada

1776.

321 St. Andrew's L. Robin Hood, Charles ft. St. James's, 4th M.

322 Royal York L. of Perfeverance, Coldftream Reg. of Guards, 1ft F.

323 *L. of Concord, at the Guildhall, Southampton,* 1ft *F. Sum.* 1ft and 3d *F. Win.*

324 *Royal Oak L. at the Royal Oak, Rippon, Yorkfhire, laft S. Sum.* 2d and laft *S. Win.*

325 L. of Honour, Bell, York ft. Weftminfter, 1ft Tu.

326 *Induftrious L. at the King's Head Inn, Canterbury,* 1ft and 3d *Th.*

328 *King of Pruffia, Penrith, in Cumberland,* 2d *W.*

329 *L. of United Friendfhip, Falcon Tav. Gravefend,* 2d & 4th *Th.*

1777.

330 L. of the Nine Mufes, Thatched Houfe Tav. St. James's ftr. 2d F.

331 *Union L. Golden Lion, Thurfday Market, York,* 1ft & 3d *M.*

332 *Social L. White Hart, Bocking, Effex, M. on or preceding full M.*

333 *Gnoll L. Ship and Caftle, Neath, Glamorganfhire,* 1ft and 3d *Tu.*

334 L. in the Ifland of Nevis

335 In the 6th, or Innifkilling Reg. of Dragoons

1778.

337 L. at Meffina, in Sicily

1779.

338 *Northumberland L. private Room, Alnwick, Northumberland,* 2d *M.*

339 L. of Independence, Vine Tav. Broad ft. Ratcliff, 3d Tu.

340 Pilgrim L. Freemafons' Tavern, Great Queen ft. laft W.

341 *L. of Fortitude, Bell Inn, Maidftone, Kent, M. nearest full M.*

1780.

342 L. of St. George, in the 1ft Reg. of Dragoon Guards, 1ft & 3d Th.

343 *St. Hild's L. private Room, S. Shields, Durham,* 2d & 4th *W.*

344 *Merchants' L. Star and Garter Tav. Liverpool,* 1ft & 3d *Th.*

345 L. at Liebau, in Courland

346 L. at Naples

K

347 St.

347 St. Michael's L. private Room, Alnwick, Northumberland, 1st & 2d M.

348 St. George's Lodge, Town Hall, Doncaster, 2d W.

1781.

349 Alfred Lodge, Wetharby, Yorkshire

351 Rodney L. Bull and Sun Inn, Kingston upon Hull, 1st & 3d Tb. Win. 1st Tb. Sum.

352 Lodge Friendship, private Room, Dartmouth, Devonshire, 1st, 3d, and last, Tb.

353 L. of Moral Reformation, Gun Tav. Deptford, 2d M.

354 La Loggia della Verita, Naples

355 Hiram's L. Ship Tav. Leadenhall street, last M.

1782.

356 St. George's E. York Militia L. in E. Riding Reg. of York Militia

357 Lodge of Science, Spread Eagle Inn, Salisbury, 1st F. Win.

358 Old British and Ligurian L. Genoa

359 Mount Sinai L. St. John's, Antigua

360 L. of True Love & Unity, Brixham, Devon, 1st and 3d W.

361 L. of Peace. Joy, and Brotherly Love, Penryn, Cornwall

1783.

362 Mariners' L. New Dock, Liverpool, 1st and 3d Tb.

363 Minerva L. Hull, Yorkshire

364 L. of Good Intention, in North, or 2d, Reg. of Devon Militia, 1st and 3d W.

365 Loyal L. Globe Inn, Barnstaple, 1st and 3d Tb.

366 Apollo L. Parade Coffee House, Salisbury, 2d and 4th W.

1784.

367 L. at Placentia, Newfoundland

368 Holmesdale L. of Freedom and Friendship, Bell, Ryegate, Surrey

369 Harmonic L. Bush Inn, Dudley, Worcestershire, 2d & 4th Tb.

370 African L. Boston, New England

371 Lodge of Truth, Cricketters, Richmond Green, 2d & 4th Tb.

372 Raby L. Raby Castle, Staindrop, Durham, 2d Tu.

1785.

373 Royal Gloucester Lodge, Bell Inn, Gloucester

374 L. of Concord, Old King's Arms, Plymouth Dock

375 La Parfaite Amitié, at Avignon, Languedoc

376 St. John's L. at Michilimacinac, Canada

377 Barry L. in the 34th Regiment

378 Rainsford L. in the 44th Regim.

379 Tyrian L. at the George Inn, Derby

381 Harbour Grace, Newfoundland

382 Trinity L. Golden Lion, Coventry, 1st & 3d Tb.

383 L. of Unanimity, private Room, Sadler st. Wells, Somersetshire, 1st & 3d Tb.

384 L. of Harmony, private Room, Hampton Court, occasional

385 L. of St. George, White Hart, New Windsor, Berks

386 Thanet L. Parade Hotel, Margate, 2d and 4th W.

387 L. of Good Intent, Ship Tavern, Leadenhall st. 2d W.

388 White Lion, Whitchurch, Shropsh. Tb. previous to the full Moon

389 L. of Perfect Friendship, King's Head, King's st. Ipswich, 3d W.

390 Lodge of Unions, Spread Eagle, Pratt st. Lambeth, 1st M.

1786.

391 L. of Independence, Castle and Falcon, Watergate st. Chester

392 L. of Benevolence, Antelope Inn, Sherborn, Dorset, 1st & 3d Tb.

394 L. of Friendship and Sincerity, Red Lion Inn, Shaftesb. Dorset, 1st and 3d Tb.

395 Phœnix L. private Room, Portsm. occasional

396 L. of the Black Bear, in the City of Hanover, (have met since 1774)

397 St. John's L. Golden Cross, Broomsgrove, Worcestersh. 2d & 4th M.

398 Carnatic Military L. at Velloro, No. 2, Coast of Coromandel

400 Hiram's L. at Gibraltar

401 L. of Goodwill, private Room, Braintree, Essex

402 L. of Sincerity, at the Buck and Vine, Wigan, Lancashire

403 L. of Harmony, at the Ship, Ormskirk, Lancashire

404 Snowden L. at the Sportsman, Carnarvon, N. Wales

1787.

405 L. of St. Charles, at Hildburghausen

406 St. Matthew's L. Barton upon Humber

407 Amphibious Lodge, at the Marine Barracks, Stonehouse, near Plymouth

408 Newtonian L. Elephant & Castle, Knaresborough, 4th M.

410 L. of Trade & Navigation, New Eagle & Child, Northwich, Cheshire, 1st W.

411 L. of Unity, Three Crowns Inn, Litchfield, st & 3d M.

412 Prince of Wales's Lodge, Star and Garter, Pall Mall

413 L. Astrea, at Riga, with permission to assemble in the Dutchy of Courland

414 Royal

414 *Royal Denbigh* L. at the Crown Inn, at Denbigh, N. Wales
415 L. Absalom, have since met since 1740, at Hambourg
416 L. St. George, ditto 1743; at ditto
417 L. Emanuel, ditto 1774, at ditto
418 L. Ferdinand Caroline, ditto 1776, at ditto
419 L. of Perfect Harmony, St. Thomas Mount, No. 3, Coast of Coromandel
420 L. of Social Friendship, at Madras, No. 4, ditto
421 L. at Trichinopoly, No. 5, ditto
422 L. of Social Friendship, St. Thomas Mount, No. 6, ditto
423 *Prince of Wales's* L. White Hart, Gainsborough, Lincolnshire, 3d M.
424 St. Paul's L. Montreal, Canada
425 In the Regiment of Anhalt Zerbst
426 L. of Unity, at Fort William Henry, in Canada
427 St. James's L. at Cataraqui, in ditto
428 Select L. at Montreal, in ditto
429 New Oswegatchie L. in ditto
430 St. John's L. at Niagara, in ditto
1788.
432 *Wiltshire* L. at the Black Swan, Devizes, Wiltshire
433 L. of Unanimity, George Inn, Ilminster, Somersetshire, Tu. before full Moon
434 Salopian L. at the Fox, in Shrewsbury, 1st Tu.
435 Bank of England L. Guildhall Coffee House, King st. Cheapside, 4th Th.
436 L. of Honour and Perseverance, Ship, Cockermouth, Cumberland, 1st Th.
437 Philanthropic L. Cock & Bell Inn, Milford, Suffolk, Tu. preceding or on full Moon
438 Duke of York's L. White Bear Inn, Doncaster, 1st M.
439 Royal Yorkshire L. Devonshire Arms, Kighley, Yorkshire, 1st M.
440 The Old Globe L. Old Globe Inn, Scarborough
441 Lodge of Naphtali, New Market Inn, Manchester
442 L. of Unity, Royal Oak, Manchester
443 L. of Union, St. John's Tavern, Manchester
444 L. of Fidelity, Thorn Inn, Burnley, Lancashire
1789.
445 *Egerton* L. Red Lion Inn, Whitchurch, Shropshire
446 Star and Garter, Pall Mall
447 L. of Unity, at Dantzick

448 St. John's Lodge of Secrecy and Harmony, at Malta
449 County Stewards' L. Freemasons' Tavern, Great Queen st.
450 At Frederickton, New Brunswick, N. America
451 *Cambrian* L. at the Swan Inn, Brecon, S. Wales, 3d M.
452 *Royal Clarence* L. White Horse, Brighthelmstone, Sussex, 3d and 4th M.
453 L. of Harmony, at the White Hart, in the Drapery, Northampton
454 Beneficent L. at the Angel, Macclesfield, Cheshire
455 *Royal York* Lodge, Bush Tavern, Corn st. Bristol, 1st and 3d W.
456 L. Frederick Charles Joseph, of the Golden Wheel, at Mentz
457 *Wrekin* L. at the Pheasant, Wellington, Shropshire, M. previous to full Moon
458 L. of Tranquillity, Old Bear's Head, Manchester
459 Independent L. at the Black Lion and Swan, Congleton, Cheshire
460 Albion L. at Skipton, Yorkshire
461 L of Harmony, Bacchus, Halifax, Yorkshire, 2d M.
462 L. Good Fellowship, Saracen's Head, Chelmsford, Essex, F. on or preceding full Moon
463 L. of Friendship, at the Angel, Oldham, Lancashire
464 L. of the North Star, at Fredericksnagore, 7th L. of Bengal
465 Calpean L. at Gibraltar
1790.
466 Friendly L. King's Head Tavern, Holborn, 2d Th.
468 Harmony L. Dolphin Hotel, Chichester, Sussex
469 *Royal Clarence* L. George Inn, Frome, Somerset
470 Corinthian L. at the Ram Inn, Newark, Nottinghamshire, M. near full Moon
471 St. John's L. at the Lion and Dolphin, Market-place, Leicester, 1st W.
472 L. Archimedes, of the Three Tracing Boards, Altenburg, Germany
473 L. of the Three Arrows, at Nurnberg, ditto
474 L. of Constancy, at Aix la Chapelle, ditto
475 L. of the Rising Sun, at Kempton, in Swabia, ditto
476 L. of the Temple of True Concord, at Cassel, ditto
477 L. Charles of Unity, at Carlsruhe, ditto
K 2   478 L.

478 L. of Perfect Equality, at Crey-
feld, ditto

479 L. Aftrea, of the Three Elms, at
Ulm, ditto

480 L. St. Charles of the Red Tower,
at Ratifbon, ditto

481 L. of Solid Friendfhip, at Trichinopoly, No. 7, Coaft of Coromandt

482 Lodge of Benevolence, Red Lion,
Stockport, Chefhire

483 Rein Deer Inn, Worcefter, 2d and
4th Th.

484 Lodge of Fortitude, at the Golden
Shovel, Lancofter

1791.

485 Silurean L. King's Head Inn,
Kington, Herefordfhire

486 L. of Friendfhip, Gibraltar

487 Bedford L. King's Arms, Taviftock,
Devonfhire, 1ft and 3d W.

488 Lodge of Amity, Swan Inn, Roch-
dale, Lancafhire

489 At Abrifluith, South Wales

490 L. of the Silent Temple, at
Hildefheim, in Germany

491 Doric L. Ship Tavern, Grantham,
Lincolnfhire, 2d F.

492 St. John's L. at the Talbot,
Henley in Arden, Warwickfhire,
1ft and 3d F.

493 Loyal and Prudent L. Leeds,
Yorkfhire

494 Lodge of Love and Harmony,
Barbadoes.

1792.

495 At Bulam, on the Coaft of Africa

496 North Nottinghamfhire L. Town
Hall, Eaft Retford, 2d F.

497 Lodge of St. George, at a private
Room, North Shields, Northumberland

498 Rawdon L. between the Lakes in
Upper Canada

499 Faithful L. at Biddeford, Devon

500 L. of Prudence, at the Three
Tuns, Halefworth, Suffolk

501 Man and Moon, St. Mary's,
Norwich

502 L. of Love and Honour, Bell Inn,
Shipton Mallet, Somerfet, 2d and
4th Tu. Win. 2d Tu. Sum.

503 Royal Gloucefter L. Eaft ftreet,
Southampton

504 Samaritan L. at the Devonfhire
Arms, Kighly, Yorkfhire

505 Philanthropic L. Devonfhire Arms,
Skipton, Yorkfhire

506 L. of the Three Graces, Barnoldf-
wick, in Craven, Yorkfhire, 2d Sa.

507 Bermuda L. at St. George's, in
Bermuda

508 Noah's Ark L. Canal Coffee Houfe,
Middlewich, Chefhire

509 L. of Unanimity, Stockport, Chefhire,
1ft W. after full Moon

510 Urania L. Angel Inn, Glamford
Briggs, Lincolnfhire

511 L. of Harmony, Black Dog, New-
church, Roffendale, Lancafhire

512 Lodge of Fidelity, White Horfe,
Bear-lane, Leeds

1793.

513 White Hart, Huddersfield, Yorkfhire

514 Union Lodge, Rofe. Edgbafton ft.
Birmingham, W. on or before full
Moon

515 Cambridge New Lodge, Red Lion,
Cambridge

516 Shakefpear L. White Lion, Strat-
ford upon Avon, Warwickfhire

517 Rural Philanthropic L. Highbridge
Inn, Huntfpill, Somerfetfhire, Tu.
preceding full Moon

518 At the Caftle, Lord ft. Liverpool

519 Scarfdale L. Angel Inn, Chefterfield,
Derbyfhire

520 The King's Friends Lodge, Three
Pigeons, Nantwich, Chefhire

521 Union L. at Cornwall, in Upper
Canada

522 St. John's L. of Friendfhip, at
Montreal

523 Friendly Brothers L. at the
Buck, Newcaftle, Staffordfhire
1ft W.

524 L. of Urbanity, Bear Inn, Win-
canton, Somerfetfhire, 1ft F.

525 Conftitutional L. at the Tiger,
Beverley, Yorkfhire

526 Union L. Macclesfield, Chefhire
1ft Th.

527 Royal Brunfwic Lodge, Royal Oak,
Sheffield, Yorkfhire

528 At Chunar in the Eaft Indies, 8th
Lodge of Bengal

529 L. of Mars, Cawnpore, 9th Lodge
of Bengal

530 Witham L. Rein Deer Inn, City
of Lincoln

531 L. of Unity, Half Moon, Market-
place, Yarmouth, Norfolk, M.
neareft full Moon

532 L. of Harmony, Blue Ball, Roch-
dale, Lancafhire

533 Royal Edward Lodge, Red Lion,
Leominfter, Herefordfhire, 2d M.

534 L. of St. John, at the Grapes,
Lancafter

1794.

535 Lodge of Emulation, Marquis of
Granby, Dartford, Kent, Tu.
neareft full Moon

536 L. of Minerva, King's Arms,
Afton under Line, Lancafhire

537 The

(71)

537 *The Apollo Lodge, Angel, Alcester, Warwickshire, 1st and 3d W.*
538 *L. of Unity and Friendship, New Bear Inn, Bradford, Wilts*
539 *L. of Hope, at the Duke of York, Bradford, Yorkshire*
540 *Benevolent L. at the Newfoundland Fishery, Teignmouth, Devon*
541 *L. in Cheshire Militia*
542 *Philanthropic Lodge, Crown Inn, Kirkgate, Leeds*
543 *Crown Inn, Nantwich, Cheshire, Th. near full Moon*
544 *Apollo L. White Lion, Beccles, Suffolk*

1795.

545 *L. of St. Winifred, King's Head, Holywell, Flintshire*
546 *Alfred L. private Room, Leeds*
547 *St. Bartholomew's L. White Lion, Fazley, Tamworth, Staffordshire, 2d Tu.*

548 *L. of Peace & Good Neighbourhood, Wynnstay, Denbighshire*

1796.

549 *Loyal Halifax L. King of Bells, Halifax, Yorkshire, 3d M.*
550 *L. of Prince George, White Lion, Masworth, Yorkshire, 1st W.*
551 *L. of Harmony, Fountain Tavern, Gosport*
552 *Perfect L. Horse and Star, Woolwich*
553 *L. of Strict Benevolence, Maid's Head, Lynn, Norfolk*
554 *Vectis L. of Peace and Concord, Wheat Sheaf, Newport, Isle of Wight, 2d M.*
555 *Union L. Grapes Inn, Carlisle*
556 *Ebenezer L. Partly Bridge, Yorkshire*
557 *South Saxon L. Star Inn, Lewes, Sussex*

Tables of the Town, Country, and Foreign, Lodges, with Reference to the Numerical List, by the Number of each Lodge.

TOWN-LODGES, according to their Days of Meeting.

M O N D A Y S.

1st.—5, 21, 180, 203, 238.
1st. & 3d.—18.
2d.—26, 322, 327, 380.
3d. & 4th.—2, 228.

3d.—7, 12, 110, 188, 249, 390.
4th.—20, 30, 50, 186, 242, 321.
Last.—355.

T U E S D A Y S.

1st.—135, 283, 325.
1st. & 3d.—4, 90, 142.
3d.—43, 95, 104, 178, 182, 231.

2d. and 4th.—32.
3d.—92, 183, 211, 339.

W E D N E S D A Y S.

1st.—134, 205, 236.
1st. & 3d.—1, 6, 57, 263.
2d.—29, 54, 68, 96, 258, 387.
2d. & 4th.—3, 257.

3d.—8, 113, 218.
4th.—55, 66, 117, 118,
Last.—340.

T H U R S D A Y S.

1st.—14, 21, 25, 41, 49, 72, 97, 217, 287.
2d.—67, 215, 239, 264, 466.

2d. & 4th.—9, 23, 53.
3d.—128, 131, 169, 184.
4th.—60, 69, 435.

F R I D A Y S.

1st.—171.———2d.—330.———3d.—27.———4th.—124.

TOWN

(72)

TOWN LODGES.

Bishopfgate ftr. 113
Bloomfbury High ftr. 218
Carnaby fq. 4
Cavendifh fq. 7
Cateston ftr. 12
Chancery lane, 20
Cheapfide, King ftr. 280,
435
Covent Garden, 231
Clerkenwell, 263
Char ng Crofs, 134
Doctor's Comm. 18, 30
Eaft Smithfield, 29, 41
Fleet ftr. Silver ft. 15
———— Shoe lane, 264
Fifh ftr. Hill, 60
Great Queen ftr. 1, 2, 21,
23, 96, 205, 340, 449
Grofvenor fq. Brook ftr.
8, 68, 124
———— Mount ftr. 60
Goodmans F. Manfel ftr.
25
Haymarket, 71
Holborn, 14, 184, 217, 466

Iflington, 283
Lambeth Marfh, 50
———— Pratt ftr. 390
Leadenhall ftr. 53, 355,
387
Ludgate Hill, 242, 259
Limehoufe, 257
Oxford ft. Old Cavendifh
ftr. 95
———— N. Audley ft. 97
———— Wells ftr. 188
Old ftr. Road, 118
———— Square, 185
Piccadilly, Dover ftr. 22,
———— Marybone ftr. 32
———— Halfmoon ftr. 69
———— Air ftr. 110
———— Burlington ftr. 128
Pall Mall, 27, 412, 446
Paddington, 55
Portland Road, 185
Rathbone Place, 182
Ratcliff, Broad ftr. 339
St. James's ftr. 3, 26, 54,
117, 171, 238, 330

St. James's ftr. Charles ftr.
321
Spitalfields, 169
Strand, Surry ftr. 43
Southwark, Joiner ftr. 66
———— Horfeydown la. 67
———— Tooley ftr. 178
———— Shad Thames, 203
———— Chriftchurch, 211
———— Bermondfey, 218, 231
———— St. Saviour's C. Y.
258
Soho, Old Compton ftr.
215
Smithfield, 287
Temple Bar, 236
Weftminfter, Palace Yd. 5
———— Downing ftr. 92
———— Crown ftr. 104
———— Whitehall, 186
———— York ftr. 325
Wapping, 9, 57
Whitechapel, Red Lion ft.
242
Walworth, 249

COUNTRY LODGES.

BERKSHIRE.

New Windfor	— — —	385	

CAMBRIDGESHIRE.

Cambridge	106 515	Ifle of Ely	179

CHESHIRE.

Chefter	58, 123, 207, 391	Congleton	459
		Stockport	482 509
Nefton	253	Middlewich	508
Northwich	410	Nantwich	520 543
Macclesfield	454, 526	Chef. Militia	561

CORNWALL.

Falmouth	87	Scilly	235
Redruth	103	Penryn	361

CUMBERLAND.

Carlifle	273, 555	Penrith	328
Workington	312	Cockermouth	436

DERBYSHIRE.

Derby	379	Chefterfield	519

DEVONSHIRE.

Exeter	35, 146	Paignton	277
Plymouth	79, 137, 140	Dartmouth	352
		Brixham	360
Stonehoufe	407	Devon. Militia	364
Plymouth D.	254, 268, 374	Barnftaple	365
		Tavistock	487
Newt Ab.	141, 243	Biddeford	499
Topfham	177	Teignmouth	540
Tiverton	226		

DORSETSHIRE.

Pool	187	Sherborn	392
Dorchefter	310	Shaftefbury	394

DURHAM.

Stockton	19	BarnardCaftle	262
Swalwell	44	Gatefhead	295
Sunderld	121, 129	S. Shields	343
Darlington	144	Staindrop	372
Old Elvit	166		

ESSEX

(73)

FOREIGN

(74)

FOREIGN LODGES.

New Orleans Scottish Rite College

http://www.no-sr-college.com

Clear, Easy to Watch
Scottish Rite and Craft Lodge
Podcast & Video Education